Private Pilot Maneuvers Manual

JEPPESEN
SANDERSON

JS314302C

INTRODUCTION

The new *Maneuvers Manual* is an authoritative operational guide designed for private pilot flight training under revised FAR Parts 61 and 141. It provides the student with the knowledge necessary to perform the maneuvers and procedures listed in the Private Pilot Flight Test Guide. The manual also will benefit certificated private and commercial pilots who wish to update their skills with refresher training or to complete their biennial flight review.

The *Maneuvers Manual* is a flight training reference and should be studied prior to the introduction of new maneuvers and procedures in the airplane. Your instructor will designate the areas that you should become familiar with as your training progresses. It will be of benefit to continue to review previously studied areas throughout your training program so that you will be thoroughly prepared for the flight test.

The sequence of subject areas presented in the manual generally is designed around the chronological order that new maneuvers and procedures are introduced. Depending on the type of program you are enrolled in, it may be necessary to vary the sequence of study.

The *Maneuvers Manual*, in conjunction with the other Private Pilot Course components, will provide an effective, practical approach to your training program. Pilots who complete this course of study will be well qualified to meet the private pilot certification requirements specified in the Federal Aviation Regulations.

TABLE OF CONTENTS

PART II — WORKBOOK

chapter 1

PRIMARY MANEUVERS

INTRODUCTION

The first step in mastering a new skill is learning the fundamentals involved in that skill. In flying, this requires a thorough understanding of and high level of proficiency in straight-and-level flight, climbs, descents, and turns. All other flight maneuvers and procedures are combinations of these four fundamentals. The training of every pilot must begin with mastery of these fundamentals; his progress through a flight training program depends on this foundation.

SECTION A - STRAIGHT-AND-LEVEL FLIGHT

LEVEL FLIGHT

Flight training normally begins with instruction in the techniques of straight-and-level flight. The objectives of straight-and-level flight are to point the airplane in a particular direction, maintain that direction, and fly at a predetermined altitude. Since no one can maintain perfectly straight-and-level flight, this maneuver can be defined as a series of recoveries from slight climbs, descents, and turns.

The pilot controls the airplane's direction and altitude by controlling the nose and wing positions in reference to the natural horizon. This is called *attitude flying*. During training in attitude flying, the pilot learns that there is a fixed nose position, or pitch attitude, and a fixed wing position, or bank attitude, with respect to the horizon for each flight condition. With a constant power setting and the aircraft's attitude adjusted to these fixed positions, the aircraft will maintain the selected flight conditions.

The pilot should be aware of the difference between—*visual flying* and *instrument flying*. Visual flying simply means that the natural horizon is used as a reference point. Instrument flying is performed when the pilot refers to the flight instruments for airplane attitude reference. This reference information is derived from the attitude indicator (artificial horizon), altimeter, and the heading indicator. Visual and instrument references for straight-and-level flight are depicted on figure 1-1.

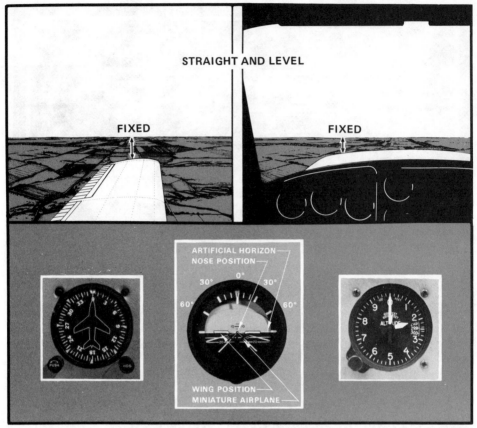

Fig. 1-1. References for Straight-and-Level Flight

CONTROLLING BANK ATTITUDE

In straight-and-level flight, the wings remain level with the horizon and the fuselage is parallel to the earth's surface. To maintain this configuration, it is necessary to fix the relationship of the airplane with the horizon. To do this, the pilot picks a point on the wingtip for a reference and the wings-level position is maintained by keeping the wingtips a given distance above or below and parallel to the horizon. Figure 1-2 shows how the wings-level attitude looks in relation to the horizon in a low wing and a high wing airplane.

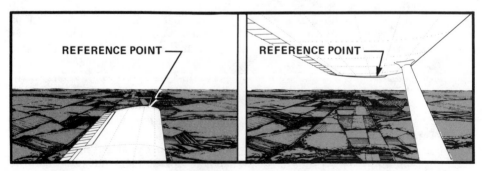

Fig. 1-2. Wing References for Level Flight

CONTROLLING PITCH ATTITUDE

To control pitch attitude, or nose position, the pilot selects a point on the airplane's nose or a spot on the windshield as a reference point. As shown in figure 1-3, this point should be *directly in front of the pilot*, rather than over the center of the airplane's nose. If the pilot sights directly over the center of the nose to a point on the horizon, the airplane will be placed in a skid. The exact appearance of the wingtips and nose in reference to the horizon depends on the type of airplane being flown, the height of the pilot, and how he positions his seat.

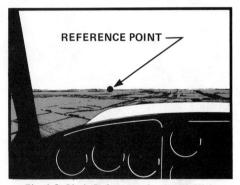

REFERENCE POINT

Fig. 1-3. Pitch References for Level Flight

The key element in attitude flying is determination of the attitude that results in level flight; that is, the wing and nose positions with respect to the horizon. These positions always remain the same as long as the pilot sits in the same position in the same type of airplane.

CONTROLLING HEADING AND ALTITUDE

In practicing straight-and-level flight, the pilot learns to maintain a specific compass heading and establishes the wing and nose attitudes for level flight, then periodically refers to the heading indicator and altimeter to verify that he is on the desired heading and at the preselected altitude.

ATTITUDE FLYING

To fly by instrument reference, the pilot must learn the techniques of *scanning*. He should develop the habit of keeping his eyes moving continuously between reference points and observing other air traffic in his vicinity. As shown in figure 1-4, the eye should move from one wing, to the nose, to the appropriate instruments, and then to the other wing. At no time should the pilot concentrate entirely on any one reference.

Several forces may cause the airplane to drift from the desired attitude. Power changes, turbulence, wind gusts, and brief periods of inattention to wing position all can cause changes in heading or altitude.

Since flying is a *continuous* series of small corrections, the pilot must learn to maintain the correct attitude as closely as possible and make smooth, prompt corrections, as necessary. Abrupt changes can result in overcorrection of the deviation.

Fig. 1-4. Visual and Instrument References

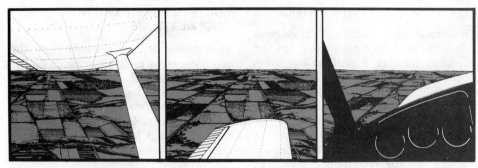

Fig. 1-5. Left Wing Low and Nose Level

The corrections should always be made in two steps. *First*, the *attitude deviation* is stopped. If the heading is changing or the altitude is changing, control pressures are applied to return to the level flight attitude. *Second*, the attitude reference points are adjusted to make a *slow correction* back to the desired readings and the power setting is adjusted, if required. After the corrections are made, the pilot should return to the normal attitude references.

Some examples of how the airplane's nose and wing positions look when the attitude is slightly divergent from straight and level are shown in figure 1-5 and 1-6. In figure 1-5, the left wing is low and the nose is level. In figure 1-6, the left wing is high and the nose is high.

The nose position helps the pilot tell when the wings are not level. The position of the wingtip also provides a small clue when the nose is high or low.

In each position, the pilot should return the airplane to a straight-and-level atti-

tude, then check the heading indicator and altimeter and note the amount of correction necessary. Finally, he should make a very small attitude change to bring the instruments back to the desired readings.

ALTITUDE AND ELEVATOR MOVEMENT

Changes in pitch attitude, caused by movement of the elevator, result in altitude changes during cruising flight. The elevator also affects the rate of climb or descent during altitude changes. Since it controls the pitch position of the nose, it can be said that altitude is controlled primarily by the elevator in straight-and-level flight.

AIRSPEED AND POWER

After the pilot gains reasonable control over the airplane attitude (altitude control), he is able to control airspeed primarily with power. When power is variable, the throttle is used primarily to control airspeed and the elevator (or stabilator) to control altitude. (See Fig.

Fig. 1-6. Left Wing High and Nose High

Fig. 1-7. Elevator Primarily Controls Altitude; Throttle Primarily Controls Airspeed

1-7.) However, after airspeed has been established at cruise airspeed and power is constant, it is possible to use airspeed variations to detect pitch attitude changes. As illustrated in figure 1-8, if the nose is high, the airspeed is slower than cruise; if the nose is low, the airspeed is higher than cruise. If the nose is moving, the airspeed is changing; if the nose is steady, the airspeed is steady.

TRIM

Trim adjustments eliminate the need for continuous forward or back pressure on the elevator to maintain attitude. If the airplane feels nose heavy, the pilot is holding back pressure to maintain a given attitude. As illustrated in figure 1-9, he should move the elevator trim control to lessen the required pressure

Fig. 1-8. Airspeed is Sensitive to Pitch when Power is Constant

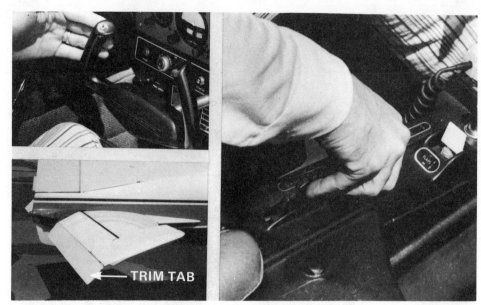

Fig. 1-9. Trim Tab Relieves Control Pressures

until he arrives at a setting which requires *no pressure* to maintain the proper attitude.

The trim tab is used only to remove control wheel pressure; it is not used to fly the airplane. The proper procedure is to set the airplane in the desired pitch attitude and at the selected airspeed, then trim away any control pressure necessary to hold that attitude. Trim tab adjustments should be made whenever the pilot changes airspeed, attitude, or power and wants to maintain the new configuration for even a short time.

EFFECTS OF RUDDER USE

Airplanes are designed to remain in stable, aerodynamic balance during cruising flight. Therefore, aileron or rudder pressures are not required constantly. This balanced condition is sometimes referred to as flying "hands off," meaning the pilot can remove his hands and feet from the controls and the airplane continues flying straight.

During normal flight, the rudder is streamlined with the airflow over the airplane, and the ball of the turn coordinator or turn-and-slip indicator remains in the center of the inclinometer. If the ball moves out of the center, the airplane is skidding or slipping. Rudder pressure should be applied to return the ball to the center.

A rule for rudder correction is, "When the ball is out of the center, *step on the ball.*" In other words, rudder pressure is applied to the side toward which the ball has moved. In figure 1-10, the ball is to the left of center, so left rudder pressure is applied.

STRAIGHT-AND-LEVEL FLIGHT BY INSTRUMENT REFERENCE

After practicing straight-and-level flight using visual references, the student repeats this practice using only instrument references. The airplane responds and reacts just as when it is flown using visual references. During flight by instrument reference, attitude flying is still practiced, utilizing the attitude indicator, airspeed indicator, vertical velocity

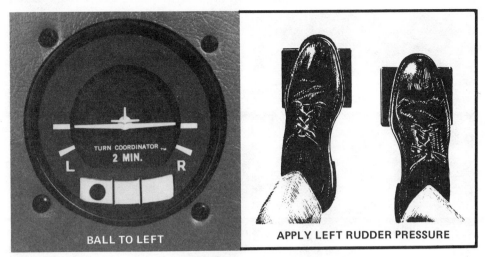

BALL TO LEFT

APPLY LEFT RUDDER PRESSURE

Fig. 1-10. Rudder Use to Correct Skid or Slip

indicator, and altimeter for pitch control, and the turn coordinator and heading indicator for heading control. (See Fig. 1-11.)

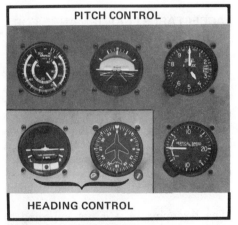

PITCH CONTROL

HEADING CONTROL

Fig. 1-11. Flight Instruments

In most modern airplanes, flight instruments are arranged in a basic "T" configuration, with the attitude indicator as the center of the "T" and supporting instruments beside and below. This arrangement, shown in figure 1-12, makes it easier for the pilot to scan the instruments.

The attitude indicator supplies the pilot with both bank attitude and pitch atti-

tude information. Once the airplane is established in straight-and-level flight, the student should adjust the miniature airplane in the attitude indicator so the top of the airplane is precisely in line with the top of the artificial horizon bar. If needed, the miniature airplane can be adjusted up or down to align with the horizon bar. The adjustment is made with the knob provided on the instrument.

The horizon line is designed to remain parallel to the earth's horizon to provide a substitute, or artificial, horizon. If a wing dips or the nose position changes,

Fig. 1-12. Basic "T" Instrument Arrangement

*Fig. 1-13. Left Bank and Slightly
Nose-High Attitude*

the artificial horizon moves. The attitude indicator shown in figure 1-13 indicates that the left wing is slightly low and the nose is slightly high.

Deviation from desired altitudes and headings is caused by the same forces when flying by instrument references as when using visual references, and corrections are made in the same way. When the bank attitude and heading have changed or are changing, the pilot first stops the turn by returning to the straight-and-level attitude. From the attitude indicator, the pilot's scan travels to the altimeter, and heading indicator to determine the amount of correction needed to return to the original heading and altitude. Then, he makes small attitude corrections to return to the desired readings.

KINESTHETIC SENSE

In time, the pilot develops his *kinesthetic sense*. This sense is generally defined as the feel of motion and pressure changes through nerve endings in the organs, muscles, and tendons—the feeling pilots describe as the "seat of the pants" sensation. During the student's first flight, he may not have this sense, or feel, to any great degree, but with practice he develops the kinesthetic sense.

When flying by instrument references, however, it is possible to experience *vertigo* (feelings derived from the kinesthetic sense that are not in accord with the actual attitude and heading of the airplane). These feelings can cause an inexperienced pilot to make incorrect control movements. Therefore, it is extremely important that the pilot believe *only* what his instruments tell him and not respond to his physical sensations.

ACCEPTABLE PERFORMANCE FOR STRAIGHT-AND-LEVEL FLIGHT

The minimum acceptable standards for straight-and-level flight are recognition of proper attitude using either visual or instrument references and the ability to make prompt corrections. Altitude should be maintained *within 100 feet* of assigned altitude, airspeed *within five knots* of the desired airspeed, and heading *within 10°* of the assigned heading.

The beginning pilot is not expected to perform to these standards on the first flight. However, he should strive to obtain performance that meets these tolerances as his training progresses.

SECTION B - CLIMBS AND DESCENTS

CLIMBS

When practicing climbs, the objectives are to obtain proficiency in establishing the proper climb attitude, to apply the appropriate control pressures, and to trim the airplane correctly in order to maintain the climb attitude. During practice climbs, emphasis is placed on learning the relationship between attitude and power, climb speed and climb performance.

ENTERING THE CLIMB

From straight-and-level flight, a climb is entered by increasing back pressure on the control wheel. The back pressure raises the nose of the airplane smoothly until the desired climb attitude is established. The pitch attitude, as represented by the nose position and the attitude indicator, should resemble the indications shown in figure 1-14.

As the climb attitude is established, the airspeed gradually slows and stabilizes on or near the desired climb speed. As the desired speed is approached, the pilot smoothly adds power to establish the recommended climb power setting. The combination of the climb attitude and the climb power setting determine the airplane's performance.

Since airspeed has changed, the pilot must continually hold back pressure on the control wheel in order to maintain the climb attitude. Therefore, he should make a trim tab adjustment to relieve control pressures.

The position of the wingtips and the angle which they make with the horizon can be used to assist in establishing the proper climb attitude in the same way that these indications were used to establish level flight attitudes. For example, in the left half of figure 1-15, the left wingtip is seen as it appears when the airplane is flying level for both high and low wing airplanes. By way of contrast, the same wingtip is shown in the right half of figure 1-15 when the airplane is in a climb attitude.

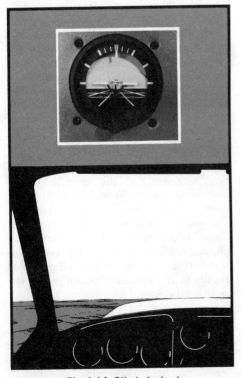

Fig. 1-14. Climb Attitude

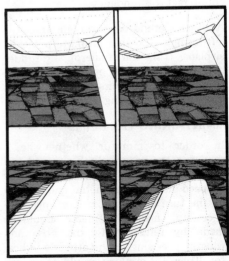

Fig. 1-15. Level Flight and Climb
Wing Tip Attitudes

The airspeed indicator serves as a primary support instrument in determining if the proper climb attitude is being maintained. If the pilot observes that the airspeed is either lower or higher than desired, he should use the available pitch attitude references to adjust the airplane's nose position, then retrim slightly when the new attitude produces the desired climb speed.

LEFT-TURNING TENDENCY DURING THE CLIMB

As the climb is established, the airplane tends to turn to the left and the ball of the turn coordinator tends to move off center to the right. This indicates that right rudder pressure is required to maintain coordination and return the ball to the center of the inclinometer.

The left-turning tendency is caused by a combination of forces, such as P-factor, torque, and spiraling slipstream. These effects are most pronounced at high power settings and low airspeeds, such as those used during climbs.

Manufacturers design airplanes to compensate for the left-turning tendency during *cruising flight*. However, at other power settings or speeds, the pilot must apply aileron and rudder pressure to counteract this tendency.

Another method used to counteract the left-turning tendency on more powerful airplanes is the use of aileron and rudder trim tabs. These tabs permit the pilot to compensate for turning effects, such as those produced during climbs.

MAINTAINING THE CLIMB

In order to monitor whether he is achieving the proper climb airspeed and heading, the pilot should refer to the airspeed indicator, altimeter, and the ball of the turn coordinator. If changes are necessary, small adjustments should be made by reference to the nose and wingtip positions or the attitude indicator. Then, the airplane should be permitted to stabilize in the new attitude and

control pressures should be removed by trimming.

CLIMB SPEEDS

In the early phases of flight training, an instructor will designate one airspeed as the *normal climb speed* and this speed will be used during the climb to practice altitude. However, before the training program has been concluded, three additional climb speeds are learned and practiced. Each of these speeds is used to achieve a different airplane performance capability.

Cruise climb speed is used to achieve a satisfactory groundspeed while climbing to cruising altitude during cross-country flight. This speed is usually higher than normal climb speed and provides adequate engine cooling, while improving forward visibility over the nose of the airplane. The pilot can determine the cruise climb speed by referring to the airplane owner's manual.

The *best rate-of-climb speed* is an important performance speed. This airspeed is lower than the cruise climb speed and provides the *most gain in altitude per minute*; therefore, it is the speed utilized to get the airplane to the desired altitude in the *shortest amount of time*, as shown in figure 1-16. The airplane does not gain altitude faster at any speed higher or lower than the designated best rate-of-climb airspeed.

The *best angle-of-climb speed* is generally the lowest of the specified climb speeds. It results in a steeper angle of climb and is used to clear obstacles in the takeoff path, such as trees or powerlines at the end of the runway. The climb profile shown in figure 1-16 illustrates that the best angle-of-climb speed results in the greatest altitude gain in the shortest distance.

LEVEL-OFF FROM A CLIMB

To return to straight-and-level flight from a climb it is necessary to begin the transition *before* reaching the desired

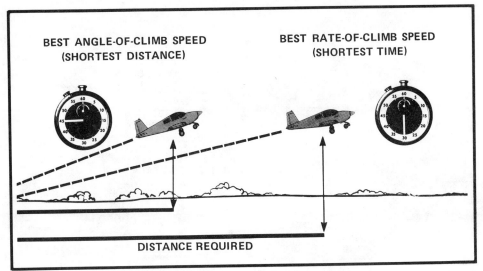

BEST ANGLE-OF-CLIMB SPEED
(SHORTEST DISTANCE)

BEST RATE-OF-CLIMB SPEED
(SHORTEST TIME)

DISTANCE REQUIRED

Fig. 1-16. Climb Speeds

altitude. The amount of lead for the leveloff depends on the rate of climb. Generally, a 10 percent lead is sufficient. For example, if the rate of climb is 500 f.p.m., the pilot should begin to level off approximately 50 feet (10 percent of 500) below the desired altitude. At that point, the nose should be smoothly lowered to the level flight attitude and this attitude should be held by visual or instrument references. (See Fig. 1-17.) Climb power is maintained until reaching cruise speed, then power is reduced to the cruise setting and control pressures required to hold the aircraft in level flight attitude are trimmed away.

ACCEPTABLE PERFORMANCE FOR CLIMBS

Acceptable performance for climbs includes prompt recognition of the proper

REDUCE ATTITUDE TO LEVEL FLIGHT

Fig. 1-17. Leveling Off from a Climb

climb attitude and proper use of the rudder and ailerons to counteract the left-turning and left-rolling tendencies. In addition, the level off must be accomplished within 100 feet of the prescribed altitude.

DESCENTS

Descents are practiced to learn the techniques used to lose altitude without gaining excessive airspeed, to control the rate of descent with power and attitude, and to convert altitude into as much distance as possible without the use of power.

Initially, descents are practiced at the *best glide speed*, which is the airspeed used for approaches to landings. After this type of descent is learned, the *cruise descent* is practiced. Since a cruise descent is flown at cruise airspeed, a higher groundspeed is maintained.

Most light training airplanes have power-off glide ratios of approximately 10 to 1. This means the airplane moves forward 100 feet for every 10 feet of altitude it loses; however, descents with power result in higher glide ratios. The ratio increases as the amount of power used during the descent increases.

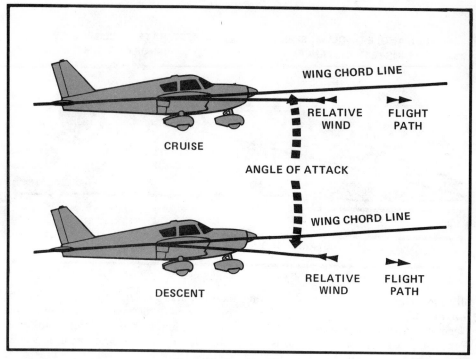

Fig. 1-18. Descent Attitude

ESTABLISHING THE DESCENT AT APPROACH SPEEDS

The first step in establishing a descent usually is to apply carburetor heat. Many airplane manufacturers recommend use of carburetor heat whenever there are prolonged periods of flight using low power settings. Next, power is reduced to a predetermined setting or to idle. As the power is reduced, back pressure is gradually applied to the control wheel until the airplane slows to the desired descent speed. When the descent airspeed is reached, the nose attitude is lowered to the descent attitude that holds this airspeed. After the proper descent attitude is established, the airplane should be trimmed.

In many airplanes the descent attitude is *nearly* the same as that used for straight-and-level cruising flight. The reason for this level descent attitude is illustrated in figure 1-18. In order to produce lift at slower airspeeds, the wing must be at a higher angle of attack. During a descent,

the higher angle of attack can be attained by maintaining a level attitude.

During the descent, the airplane experiences rolling and yawing effects *opposite* to those encountered during a climb. Therefore, small amounts of right aileron and left rudder pressure are required for proper coordination. Because the airflow over the controls is less rapid than at cruise airspeed and there is little propeller slipstream over the empennage, the controls tend to feel soft or mushy and less positive in response. The pilot can learn to use this "feel" to help determine when the airplane is flying slowly. The feel developed in practicing descents has an important application to approach and landing practice.

MAINTAINING THE DESCENT

The airspeed indicator, altimeter, heading indicator, turn coordinator, and vertical velocity indicator are used during the descent, as in other maneuvers. After the pilot has established the desired descent attitude and has the airplane trimmed properly, he should refer to these instruments to confirm that the airspeed, heading, and rate of descent are correct. If adjustment is required, he should return to the attitude clues, either visual or instrument, make an attitude adjustment, permit the attitude to stablize, and then refer to the appropriate instruments to *confirm* that he is descending as desired. For example, if back pressure is required, the desired nose attitude is established with elevator control pressure. Then, the pressures are relieved with the trim tab. If the pilot tries to establish the attitude using the trim tab rather than control pressures, he usually overcontrols the airplane, resulting in an erratic descent.

CONTROLLING THE RATE OF DESCENT

USE OF POWER

The rate of descent can be controlled with power. An increase in power decreases the rate of descent, while a decrease in power increases the rate of descent. (See Fig. 1-19.) As power is added, the pitch attitude should be held slightly higher if the pilot wishes to maintain a constant airspeed. On the other hand, a power reduction must be accompanied by lowering the pitch attitude slightly in order to maintain a given airspeed. When power is added, propeller slipstream over the elevator or stabilator increases; therefore, a small trim tab adjustment is necessary. The rate of descent can be monitored by reference to the vertical velocity indicator when the descent is well established and the instrument has settled to an accurate indication.

USE OF FLAPS

The angle of descent can be increased by the use of flaps. As flap deflection increases, it is necessary for the pilot to lower the pitch attitude, as shown in figure 1-20, if he desires to maintain a constant airspeed. Moderate trim tab adjustments also may be necessary.

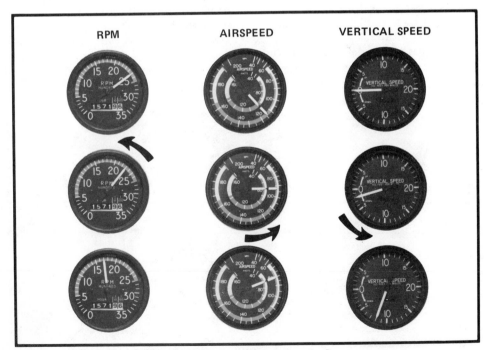

Fig. 1-19. Control of Descent Rate by Power

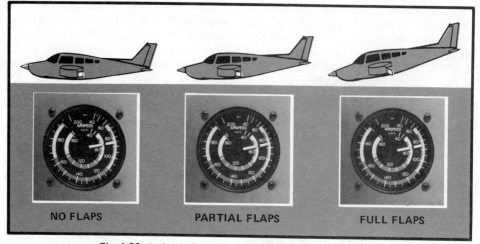

Fig. 1-20. Attitude Changes with Application of Wing Flaps

Descents with flaps retracted are made when maximum range or distance are needed. When rapid dissipation of altitude is desired, a full flap, power-off glide is used. (See Fig. 1-21.)

LEVEL-OFF FROM THE DESCENT

To return to straight-and-level flight, it is again necessary for the pilot to begin the transition to level flight before reaching the desired altitude. Approximately 50 to 100 feet above the desired altitude,

the pilot should adjust the nose position to level flight and simultaneously add power to the cruise setting. He should refer to wing and nose positions in order to maintain the proper attitude throughout the transition from descent to straight-and-level flight. Since the addition of power and the increase in airspeed produce a moderate tendency to pitch upward, the trim tab must be adjusted to relieve forward control pressures as straight-and-level flight is attained.

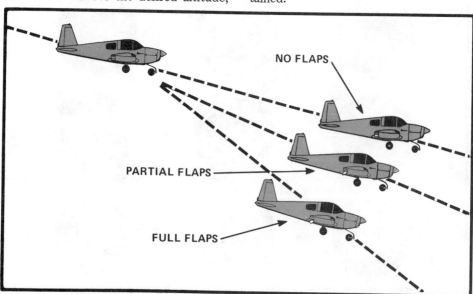

Fig. 1-21. Wing Flaps Affect Rate of Descent and Range

ACCEPTABLE PERFORMANCE FOR DESCENTS

The criteria used to evaluate acceptable descent performance is prompt recognition of the descent attitude and proper coordination of rudder and aileron pressures. Additionally, leveloffs must be within 100 feet of the desired altitude.

SECTION C - TURNS

Turns are described in general terms by the number of degrees of bank necessary to produce the turn. A *medium bank turn* is one in which the bank is approximately 30°. The medium bank normally is used for training, since most training airplanes have a tendency to return to level flight when a shallow bank is used.

WHY THE AIRPLANE TURNS

The objectives of turns are to change the direction of the airplane's flight path and develop proficiency in control coordination. Turns are made by directing a portion of the lift force of the wings to one side or the other. As shown in figure 1-22, lift is equal to weight when the airplane is in level flight. However, when the airplane turns, the lift force is tilted out of alignment with the weight and produces a force which turns the airplane. (See Fig. 1-23.) The lift force in a turn can be subdivided into two forces or components, one acting vertically and one acting horizontally. The horizontal component is the force that makes the airplane turn, while the vertical component is the force that overcomes the airplane's weight.

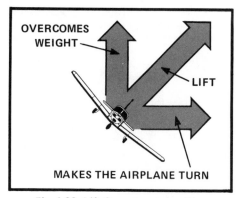

Fig. 1-23. Lift Components in a Turn

An analysis of the forces acting on an airplane in a turn is shown in figure 1-24. When the airplane is in a level turn, the vertical component of lift is opposed by an equal force, called weight, acting in the opposite direction. The horizontal component of lift, sometimes called *the turning* force, is opposed by an equal force, called *centrifugal* force, acting in the opposite direction. The total lift force created by the wings is opposed by the combination of centrifugal force and weight acting in the opposite direction. This force is termed the *resultant* force.

Since the resultant force is a combination of centrifugal force and weight, a pilot in a properly executed turn feels

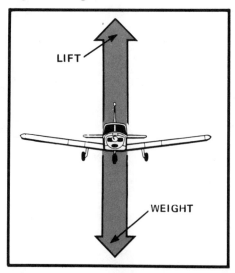

Fig. 1-22. Lift Equals Weight in Level Flight

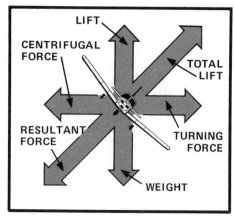

Fig. 1-24. Forces Acting on an Airplane in a Turn

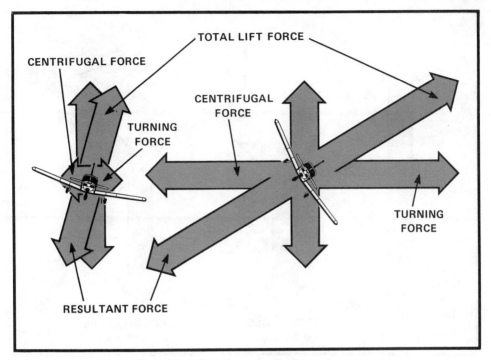

Fig. 1-25. As Bank Increases, the Forces Increase

pressed into the seat with a force somewhat greater than in straight-and-level flight. However, the pilot should experience no forces that tend to make him lean into or away from the turn.

Figure 1-25 illustrates another important concept. As the bank used to make the level turn increases, the total lift required to support the airplane and produce the turn increases. This principle is shown by the comparative lengths of the arrows indicating the turning force. For example, the arrow in the shallow bank turn is considerably shorter and of less magnitude than the arrow for the airplane making a steep bank turn. In addition, the centrifugal force is considerably greater in a steep bank turn than in a shallow bank turn. Figure 1-25 also illustrates that the resultant force, which presses the pilot into the seat, increases as the angle of bank increases.

In review, when the airplane is in level flight, the total lift force is equal to the weight, as shown on the left in figure 1-26. When the airplane is banked, the total lift force is diverted. While the total lift is still equal to the weight, the vertical component is insufficient to counteract weight and the airplane descends. Therefore, in order to maintain altitude during a turn, the total lift must be increased until the vertical component is equal to the weight. This is accomplished by increasing the angle of attack with back pressure on the control wheel.

ENTERING THE TURN

AILERON CONTROL PRESSURES

To roll into a bank, aileron control pressure is applied in the direction of the desired turn. When executing a left turn, the control pressures place the left aileron up and the right aileron down. As shown in figure 1-27, this action causes the right wing to produce more lift than the left wing, making the airplane roll to the left. How fast the airplane rolls

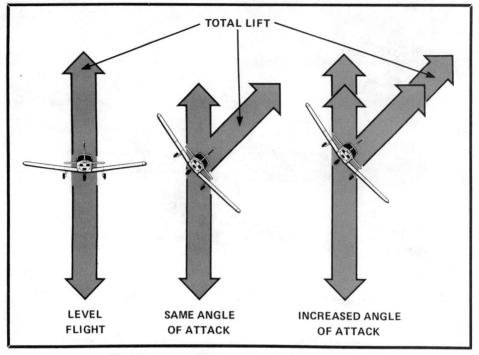

Fig. 1-26. Increased Angle of Attack Required in a Turn

depends on how much aileron control pressure is applied. How far the airplane rolls (the steepness of the bank) depends on how long the ailerons are deflected, since the airplane continues to roll as long as the ailerons are deflected. When the airplane reaches the desired angle of bank, the ailerons are neutralized.

ELEVATOR CONTROL PRESSURES

Since the pitch attitude must be increased slightly to increase the total lift when performing a turn, the nose position used to maintain the desired altitude is slightly higher in a turn than in level flight, as indicated in figure 1-28. In a medium bank turn, the required pitch attitude adjustment is slight. However, steeper banks require a much higher pitch attitude, as illustrated in figure 1-29.

Fig. 1-27. Ailerons Cause Airplane to Roll

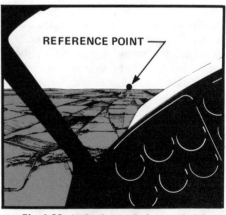

Fig. 1-28. Attitude and Reference Point in Medium-Bank Turn

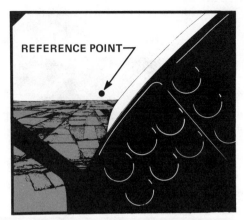

Fig. 1-29. Attitude and Reference Point in Steep-Bank Turn

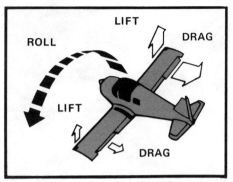

Fig. 1-30. Adverse Yaw

COORDINATION OF CONTROLS

When discussing turning techniques, pilots use the term *coordination*. This means the simultaneous application of rudder pressure each time aileron pressure is applied and application of correct elevator back pressure at the proper time.

The use of rudder pressure is made necessary by an unbalanced aerodynamic condition created when the ailerons are deflected. When the aileron is deflected downward on the right wing, as shown in figure 1-30, there is an increase in lift on that wing but the drag force also increases. The increase in drag is greater on the right wing than the increase in drag from the upward deflected left aileron. This is true because an increase in lift is always accompanied by an increase in drag and a decrease in lift is accompanied by a decrease in drag.

The increased drag on the right wing tends to make the nose move, or yaw, to the right. The production of a yaw opposite to the intended direction of turn is known as the *adverse yaw effect*. As shown in figure 1-31, it is necessary to apply just enough rudder pressure in the direction of the turn (to the left in this example) to counteract yaw. This rudder pressure is maintained as long as the ailerons are deflected; when the ailerons are neutralized, the rudder also is neutralized. The actual amount of rudder pressure necessary to counteract adverse yaw varies with different types of airplanes and is determined by practice.

The ball of the turn coordinator assists the pilot in determining how much pressure is necessary to counteract adverse yaw. For a coordinated turn, the ball should remain in the center of the inclinometer. If the ball is not in the center, as demonstrated in figure 1-32, the pilot should apply rudder pressure on the side to which the ball has rolled.

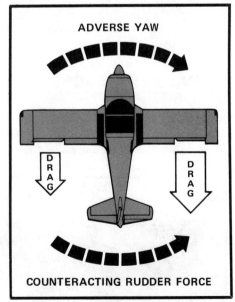

Fig. 1-31. Use of Rudder to Counteract Adverse Yaw

BALL TO LEFT—APPLY LEFT RUDDER

Fig. 1-32. "Step on the Ball"

*Fig. 1-33. Visual Reference Point Moves
with Bank Angle*

While the turn is in progress, the pilot should check the altimeter, vertical velocity indicator, and airspeed indicator occasionally to determine if corrections are necessary. If corrections are required, the pilot should make attitude adjustments in two steps. For example, if the nose is low, the airspeed high, and the altitude decreasing, pitch attitude should be increased to stop the descent and airspeed increase. When the airspeed has stopped increasing and the altitude has stabilized, the pilot should make a slight nose-up pitch attitude adjustment to return to the desired altitude.

VISUAL REFERENCES IN THE TURN

A pilot making turns by visual reference applies coordinated aileron and rudder pressures in the direction he wishes to turn. As he looks to the front, the nose of the airplane appears to move in an arc with respect to the horizon. Figure 1-33 shows that the point at which the line of sight meets the horizon should begin moving in the same direction and at the same rate as the rate and direction of bank establishment. The angle at which the cowling, instrument panel, and door posts meet the horizon assists in determining when the proper angle of bank has been attained.

The nose position appears different during left and right turns, because the pilot sits to the side of the centerline of the airplane. Both of the banks shown in figure 1-34 are approximately 15°. The one on the left looks nose-high and the one on the right looks nose-low. Therefore, the point *directly in front of the pilot's line of sight* is the point that should be used for reference during the turn.

ROLLING OUT OF THE TURN

Approximately 5° to 10° before reaching the desired heading, the pilot should

Fig. 1-34. Nose Position during Left and Right Turns

apply coordinated aileron and rudder pressures to roll out of the turn. Simultaneously, he must begin releasing the back pressure on the control wheel so aileron, rudder, and elevator pressures are neutralized when the airplane reaches the wings-level position.

TURNS BY INSTRUMENT REFERENCE

After practicing turns by visual references, the student learns to perform turns using instrument references. Control pressures are applied in the same manner as when using visual references and the indications of the instruments are interpreted similarly.

PERFORMING THE TURN

The turn by instrument reference is established in the same manner as when using visual references, except the references have changed from the wingtips and nose outside the airplane to the wing and nose positions represented on the attitude indicator. To establish a 15° banked turn, the airplane is banked until the 15° position is aligned with the bank index at the top of attitude indicator, as shown in figure 1-35. Then, aileron and rudder pressures are neutralized and the pitch attitude is adjusted slightly upward with additional back pressure on the control wheel.

Corrections are made in the same manner as when using visual references; however, the pilot adjusts the attitude by using the attitude indicator and scans the other instruments to determine that the turn is progressing as desired. One advantage of performing turns by instrument reference is that the nose position on the attitude indicator looks the same during left and right turns, as illustrated in figure 1-36. Recovery from the turn is performed by applying coordinated aileron and rudder pressure, releasing the back pressure, and reestablishing straight-and-level flight by reference to the attitude indicator.

Fig. 1-35. 15° Left Turn

Fig. 1-36. Pitch Attitude Representation for Left and Right Turns

STANDARD-RATE TURNS

The angle of bank frequently used in making turns by instrument reference is one that results in a *standard-rate turn*. A standard-rate turn produces a turn rate of *three degrees per second*. The pilot uses the turn coordinator to indicate the direction and rate of turn. As shown in figure 1-37, when the wing of the miniature airplane is aligned with the index, a standard-rate turn of 360° will be completed in two minutes. If the wing of the miniature airplane is midway between the level flight position and the standard-rate position, a one-half standard-rate turn, or a turn of 360° in four minutes, is being performed.

ANGLE OF BANK REQUIRED FOR STANDARD-RATE TURN

When an airplane is performing a standard rate turn, it will turn 3° in 1 second, 30° in 10 seconds, 90° in 30 seconds, or 180° in 60 seconds. The angle of bank necessary to produce the standard-rate turn is strictly a function of the airspeed —the greater the airspeed, the greater the angle of bank required to maintain a standard-rate turn.

Since most training airplanes maintain cruise true airspeeds of approximately

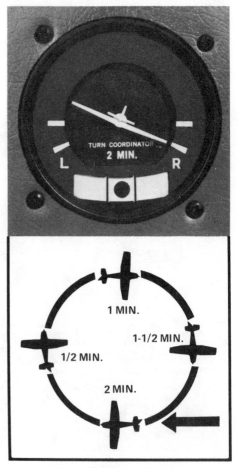

Fig. 1-37. Standard-Rate Turn

APPROXIMATE ANGLE OF BANK	TRUE AIRSPEED
15°...	100 knots
17°...	110 knots
18°...	120 knots
20°...	130 knots
21°...	140 knots
23°...	150 knots
24°...	160 knots
25°...	170 knots
26°...	180 knots
28°...	190 knots

Fig. 1-38. Angle of Bank vs. Airspeed

110 knots, the angle of bank required for a standard-rate turn is approximately 17° as shown in figure 1-38. Climbing and descending turns are normally performed at airspeeds near 100 knots. At this airspeed, a standard-rate turn requires a bank angle of 15°.

TIMED TURNS

By utilizing a standard rate, the pilot can determine the amount of time required to make a turn by instrument reference prior to initiating the turn. He should determine the number of degrees to be turned and divide by three. Then, noting the time according to the second hand on the airplane clock, he should roll into the turn using the proper angle of bank and roll out to level flight when the predetermined amount of time has elapsed. For example, to make a 180° turn, the pilot simply divides 180 by 3 and finds that it takes 60 seconds to perform this turn, as illustrated in figure 1-39.

ACCEPTABLE PERFORMANCE FOR TURNS

Acceptable performance for turns is evaluated on the basis proper coordination, smoothness, and accuracy. During turns, the selected altitude must be maintained within 100 feet and roll-out from the turn must be accomplished within 20° of the preselected heading.

COMBINATIONS OF FUNDAMENTAL MANEUVERS

Four maneuvers—straight-and-level flight, turns, climbs, and descents—are the fundamentals upon which all other flight maneuvers are based. These other maneuvers consist of combinations of

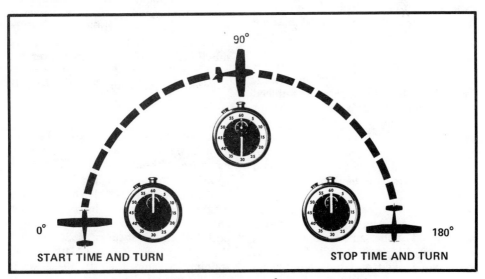

Fig. 1-39. Time Required for 180° Standard-Rate Turn

the fundamentals. If the pilot develops a thorough understanding of these basic elements and maintains effective and precise control of the airplane when performing each maneuver, he will develop a high level of proficiency as he continues his flight training.

After practicing the four fundamental maneuvers individually, the pilot practices combinations of them. Climbing and descending turns to a predetermined heading and altitude are introduced as soon as the pilot is proficient in climbs, descents, and turns. These combination maneuvers are practiced using both visual and instrument references.

CLIMBING TURNS

The objective of practicing climbing turns is to combine the techniques of climbs smoothly with those of turns. The climbing turn is used after takeoff and when climbing to a selected cruise altitude and heading.

To perform a climbing turn, the pilot should establish the climb as previously discussed. When climb power and attitude are set, he should roll to the desired bank angle. This is a two-step procedure initially; however, as the pilot gains experience and proficiency, he enters the maneuver by simultaneously establishing the climb attitude and the proper bank.

The same airspeed should be used for straight climbs and climbing turns. Therefore, the climb rate is reduced during climbing turns at a constant airspeed. Climbing turns are generally performed using shallow bank angles because a further increase in the angle of bank diverts more of the total lift and causes a further reduction in rate of climb.

The desired heading and altitude rarely are reached at the same time; therefore, if the desired heading is reached first, the wings are leveled and the climb maintained until the desired altitude is reached. On the other hand, if the altitude is reached first, the nose is lowered to a level flight attitude and the turn continued to the desired heading. If both the desired heading and altitude are reached at the same time, these procedures can be performed simultaneously.

ACCEPTABLE PERFORMANCE FOR CLIMBING TURNS

When performing climbing turns, the pilot should demonstrate proper coordination and smooth control use. He should be able to recover from the turn within 20° of an assigned heading and level off within 100 feet of an assigned altitude. The pilot should also demonstrate the prompt and effective use of trim to relieve control pressures.

DESCENDING TURNS

Descending turns to preselected headings and altitudes combine the procedures for straight descents with those used in turns. The pilot should enter the descent using either visual or instrument references in the manner previously outlined for the straight descent. When the descent attitude has been established, he should roll to the desired angle of bank. As with climbing turns, the initial procedure is performed in two steps; however, as the pilot gains proficiency, the descent attitude and bank are established simultaneously. As in any maneuver, the pilot should trim off control pressures required to maintain the selected attitude.

When using visual references, the nose looks lower in the right turn than in the left turn, although both turns are performed at the same airspeed and rate of descent. (See Fig. 1-40.) When performing descending turns by instrument references, the attitude looks the same in both left and right turns, as illustrated in the bottom half of figure 1-40. In most training airplanes, the attitude shown in the illustration produces a standard rate

Fig. 1-40. Attitudes for Descending Turns

of turn with approximately a 500 f.p.m. rate of descent.

Power is used to control the rate of descent. The pilot should make the initial power setting for the desired rate of descent and allow the pitch attitude and the rate of descent to stabilize. If a higher rate of descent is desired, power should be reduced. In contrast, the pilot must add power if the rate of descent is higher than desired.

It is recommended that the same airspeed be maintained in descending turns as in straight descents. However, the rate of descent is *higher* in a descending turn than in a straight descent with comparable power settings because the vertical lift component is less when the airplane banks. Compensation may be made with a slight addition of power.

ACCEPTABLE PERFORMANCE FOR DESCENDING TURNS

When performing descending turns, the pilot should demonstrate proper coordination and smooth control use. He should be able to recover from the turn within 20° of an assigned heading and level off within 100 feet of an assigned altitude.

COORDINATION EXERCISES

Exercises not normally required for everyday flight are utilized to develop and maintain proficiency in coordination of the flight controls. One of the most common of these exercises, called *Dutch rolls*, consists of maintaining straight-and-level flight while rolling back and forth from right to left banks without stopping at the wings-level position. As

Fig. 1-41. Dutch Rolls

shown in figure 1-41, the nose is held on a point or heading and is not allowed to rise or fall. The degree of bank at which the rolling is reversed may be shallow or steep or may vary as the maneuver is performed.

Although Dutch rolls require coordination of the rudder and ailerons in a manner *exactly opposite* to that used in normal turns, they are an excellent aid in smoothing control usage and in learning control reactions. Also, as steeper banks are used, a high degree of elevator coordination is required to keep the nose from pitching up or down in relationship to the horizon.

Another coordination exercise consists of rolling from one medium turn directly into a turn in the opposite direction, then reversing the direction again after a predetermined number of degrees of turn. For example, the turn can be reversed after 90° of turn and the airplane turned through an arc of 180°, then the direction reversed again. As proficiency is attained, the number of degrees of turn can be reduced. For example, turning 20° to 30°, then rolling into a turn in the opposite direction for 20° to 30° assists the pilot in perfecting his coordination techniques.

An advanced coordination exercise is illustrated in figure 1-42. The exercise begins when the pilot initiates a shallow 15° bank, turns right for 90°, and then turns left for 90°. The exercise is continued by rolling into a 30° banked turn, continuing this turn through 180°, and then reversing the bank and turning another 180°. The exercise is terminated by flying a 360° turn with a 45° bank followed by a similar turn of 360° in the opposite direction. Upon completion, the pilot should be on the original heading. This exercise is considered a good lead-in to advanced maneuvers.

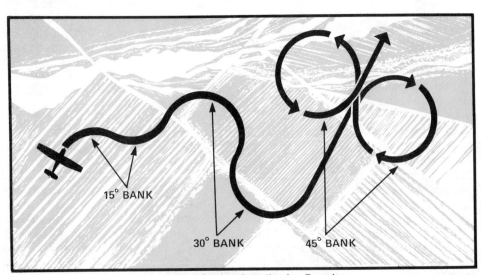

15° BANK

30° BANK

45° BANK

Fig. 1-42. Advanced Coordination Exercise

Chapter 2

AIRPLANE GROUND OPERATIONS AND TRAFFIC PATTERNS

INTRODUCTION

This chapter of the *Maneuvers Manual* is designed to introduce and explain the basics of airplane ground operation and traffic pattern procedures. Ground operations are presented in the order the pilot normally accomplishes the procedure. For example, preflight inspection is first, followed by engine starting and taxi operations. General airport traffic pattern procedures and operations also are introduced and defined; however, more in-depth coverage of traffic patterns is presented later in the text.

SECTION A - PREFLIGHT INSPECTION AND ENGINE STARTING

Safe flying begins on the ground. The attitudes and habits established in the initial stages of training greatly influence the standards that pilots follow throughout their flying careers. Students should observe their instructor carefully as the preflight and engine starting procedures are explained for the first time.

The preflight inspection is performed *prior to each flight* to ensure the aircraft is in a safe condition for the flight. The pilot in command is entirely responsible for making this decision. The flight instructor should point out the various components to be inspected and explain how to evaluate the airworthiness of an aircraft.

The airworthiness certificate is an important document for determining the condition of an aircraft. A standard certificate specifies the category (normal, utility, ac-robatic), indicates the make, model, serial number, and any exemptions from the applicable standards. The airworthiness certificate remains in effect indefinitely, as long as the aircraft is maintained and operated according to the Federal Aviation Regulations (FARs). Major alterations that appreciably change the flight characteristics must be approved by an authorized person according to the FARs. For example, a person with at least a private pilot certificate is required to flight test and approve alterations affecting flight characteristics before that aircraft may be used to carry passengers.

An aircraft that has been stored for an extended time should be preflighted with special care. Inactive aircraft frequently are used by birds, insects, and small animals as nesting places. Air ducts,

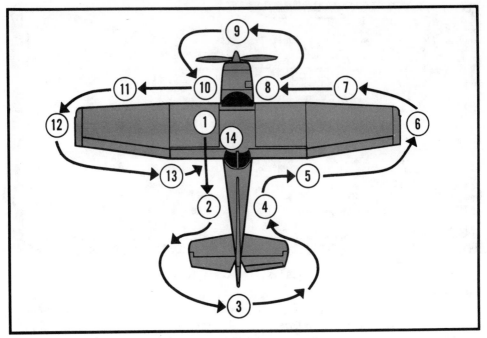

Fig. 2-1. Typical Preflight Inspection

engine baffles, and fuel tank vents are typical areas that may be obstructed by nests, eggs, or excretions. Fabric or wood also may be damaged by some insects or rodents.

CHECKLISTS

Written checklists are used because of variations in types and models of airplanes. Regardless of the number of times a procedure is repeated, the checklist should be followed step by step *to ensure that all necessary items are accomplished in a logical sequence.*

PREFLIGHT INSPECTION

The preflight inspection is only the first of many procedures that are carried out according to a written checklist. The proper sequence for a typical preflight inspection is presented in the following discussion. The numbered callouts in figure 2-1 correspond to the positions referred to in the text.

In the cabin (position 1), the *aircraft papers* are checked and should consist of the following items:

1. Weight and balance data, including equipment list (required by FAA)
2. Airplane radio station license (required by FCC)
3. Aircraft airworthiness certificate (required by FAA)
4. Aircraft registration certificate (required by FAA)
5. Engine and airframe logbooks (must be available, but not necessarily on board the aircraft)
6. Pilot's operating handbook or approved aircraft flight manual (required by FAA, if applicable)

FAR 91.31, in part, stipulates that an airplane must be operated in compliance with the operating limitations set forth in the approved flight manual. In addition to the required flight manual, specific placards and markings are prescribed by the airworthiness standards for the particular airplane type, and also must be available.

The *control lock* is removed so the controls can be checked for freedom of movement. After the master switch is turned on, the wing flaps are placed in the full down position, so the internal components can be examined.

The *fuel quantity gauges* are checked to insure proper operation and to determine the amount of fuel in each tank. Next the *windshield and cabin windows* are checked for cleanliness and general condition. The *instrument panel* is checked for any irregularities, such as cracked glass, and for any instruments or radios which might have been removed for maintenance.

When all cabin checks are completed, the *magneto switch, master switch, mixture control, and throttle* are placed in the appropriate off positions. Then, the pilot continues with the exterior portion of the preflight check.

The left portion of the *fuselage* (position 2) is checked for skin wrinkles, dents, and loose rivets. The lower surface of the fuselage is especially susceptible to rock damage and should be examined for dents, cleanliness, and evidence of excessive engine oil leakage.

The *static air source* is examined for obstruction, if located on the fuselage. During cleaning or waxing of the airplane, the small static port can be plugged with wax. It is important that the static source is open so that the airspeed, altimeter, and vertical velocity indicators function properly.

Several items are checked on the tail section (position 3). The *control surface lock*, if installed, is removed prior to checking the tail assembly. If gusty wind conditions are anticipated, external locks are often used to keep the movable control surfaces from applying heavy loads on the flight controls and the *stops* that limit the range of control movement.

The *tail surfaces* are checked for general condition, such as dents, skin wrinkles, and loose rivets. The underside and leading edge of the horizontal stabilizer or stabilator are especially prone to damage by rocks thrown up during takeoffs and landings on unimproved runway surfaces.

The *elevator* or *stabilator* and *rudder* are checked for damage, loose hinge bolts, and freedom of movement. The control cables and stops are inspected for damage and the surface skin checked for dents and wrinkles.

Several additional items are checked during this portion of the inspection. The *trim tab* is inspected for security and general condition, the *tail* and *beacon lights* are examined for damage, and the *navigation antenna* is inspected for damage. Finally, *tiedown chains* or *ropes* are removed.

If the airplane is equipped with a tailwheel, the steering arms, cables, and springs are checked for wear. In addition, the tire is inspected for wear, proper inflation, cuts, and bruises.

The right portion of the *fuselage* is inspected at position 4. The procedures used at position 2 are repeated.

The *right wing flap* and *aileron* are inspected at position 5. The *control surface locks*, if installed, are removed. The *wing flap* is inspected completely with particular attention given to all moving parts. The flap hinges are checked for security, wear, and freedom of movement. The *aileron* is examined for security, damage, and freedom of movement. In addition, the aileron pushrods or control cables are checked for security, damage, and tension.

The *right wingtip* (position 6) is checked for damage and secure attachment. Then, the *right navigation light* is inspected for damage.

The *right wing* is inspected at position 7. The *leading edge* is examined for dents or other damage and the upper wing surface is checked for frost or snow accumulation.

The *fuel tank drain* is checked for security and leakage. If the airplane is equipped with a quick-drain device, a few ounces of fuel are drained into a clear container and examined for the presence of water and other contaminants. Water can be detected because it is heavier than gasoline and settles to the bottom of the container. It contrasts clearly with the color of the gasoline. Since fuel contamination is possible at any time, this check should be accomplished prior to every flight.

The *fuel quantity level* is checked visually by removing the filler cap and looking into the tank. The quantity in the tank should agree with the fuel gauge reading observed at the beginning of the preflight inspection. At the completion of the fuel level check, the filler cap is replaced and tightened securely. Finally, the *tiedown chains* or *ropes* are removed.

The *right main landing gear* and *nose gear* are inspected at position 8. The point at which the main landing gear is attached to the fuselage or lower surface of the wing is examined for dents and wrinkles. The tires are checked for wear, cuts, bruises, and proper inflation. The wheel fairings, if installed, are inspected for cracks, dents, and general security. The hydraulic brake and brake lines are visually checked for security and leaks. Particular attention is given to proper inflation of exposed gear struts.

Several checks of the *engine* and *propeller area* are made at position 9. The *front cowl openings* are checked for obstructions. The *engine compartment*, which is accessible through the cowl access door, is inspected for loose wires and clamps, worn hoses, and oil and fuel leaks. The *cowl flaps* (if applicable) are checked for security.

The *oil quantity* is determined by removing and reading the dipstick. Oil should be added if it is below the minimum level recommended by the manufacturer. Then, the dipstick is replaced and tightened securely. The oil filler cap is checked for security.

The *fuel strainer* is drained for several seconds to eliminate any water that may have collected in the fuel strainer. Water can form in the fuel tanks from condensation of moisture in the air or it may be present in fuel added to the tanks.

The *propeller and spinner* are inspected for security and the propeller blades and tips are checked for nicks and scratches. Propeller nicks of more than approximately one-eighth inch in depth can cause excessive stress in the metal of the propeller and should be repaired by a qualified FAA licensed mechanic prior to flight.

If a constant speed propeller is installed, it is checked for oil leakage. This generally is detected by the presence of oil streaks along the propeller blade.

In cold weather, the propeller should be carefully pulled through two or three revolutions. This procedure loosens the congealed oil and makes engine starting easier.

The *cabin exterior* is examined at position 10. The *windshield and cabin windows* are checked for cleanliness and general condition. However, a dry rag should not be used to clean windshields because it can scratch the windshield surface. Only a rag and cleaning compound specifically designed for airplane windshields should be used.

The *communication antenna* is checked for general condition and security. The same procedure is used to check the *left main landing gear* as was used for the right main landing gear at position 8.

The *left wing structure* (position 11) is inspected in the same manner as the right wing (position 7). Then, the *tie-down chains* or *ropes* are removed.

The *pitot tube cover*, if installed, is removed and the tube opening is checked for obstructions. A plugged pitot tube opening causes the airspeed indicator to malfunction. In addition, the pitot tube itself should show no signs of damage and should not be bent out of alignment.

The *stall warning vane* on the leading edge of the wing is checked for freedom of movement. It is a good practice to turn the master switch on just prior to the stall warning vane inspection so that the stall warning signal can be checked when the vane is deflected upward. In the case of a pneumatic stall warning device, the leading edge opening is checked for freedom from obstructions.

Next, the *fuel tank vent* opening is checked for obstructions. The checks of the fuel tank drains, vents, and fuel quantity are performed in the same manner as described in the listing for position 7.

The *left wingtip* is examined at position 12. The procedures outlined for position 6, are repeated at this position.

The *left wing flap* and *aileron* are inspected at position 13. The procedures detailed for position 5 are repeated at this position.

The baggage door is checked at position 14. After loading the baggage, the door is closed and checked for security.

STARTING PROCEDURES

After the preflight inspection is completed, the pilot is ready to begin the prestarting checklist. Since there are a number of different procedures used to start airplane engines, use of an appropriate written checklist is important. Figure 2-2 shows an example of an engine starting checklist which is typical of those in airplane owner's manuals. The pilot should follow the recommendations of the airplane manufacturer for the best engine starting method.

Although the starting procedure can vary from airplane to airplane, there are certain common safety precautions and suggestions that apply universally. A pilot should avoid starting the engine with the tail of the airplane pointed toward parked automobiles, spectators, or an open hangar. In addition to being discourteous, it subjects persons to injury, wind blast, and debris, and property to possible serious damage.

Prior to starting the engine on an unimproved surface, the ground under the propeller should be inspected for rocks, pebbles, or any other loose debris that can be picked up by the propeller and hurled backward. Any such particles should be removed to avoid damaging the propeller and other parts of the airplane. If this is not possible, the airplane should be moved to another location before the engine is started.

STARTING THE ENGINE

(1) Carburetor Heat – COLD
(2) Mixture – RICH
(3) Primer – AS REQUIRED
(4) Throttle – OPEN 1/4 INCH
(5) Master Switch – ON
(6) Propeller Area – CLEAR
(7) Ignition Switch – START
(8) Oil Pressure – CHECK

Fig. 2-2. Typical Starting Checklist

The following discussion is based on a typical starting sequence for a training airplane. The numbered callouts refer to the items located on the control panel shown in figure 2-3.

First, the carburetor heat control (item 1) is placed in the cold position. When the control is placed in this position, the air entering the engine is filtered to remove dust and dirt. Next, the mixture control (item 2) is set to full rich.

When these settings are established, the primer (item 3) is used to pump fuel into the engine cylinders to aid in starting. The number of primer strokes required depends on the length of time the engine has been shut down and outside air temperature. If the engine has been shut down for less than an hour, it probably will start without priming. The recommended procedure, outlined in most light airplane owner's manuals, is to use from two to six strokes of the engine primer. The greater number of strokes is required when temperatures are colder.

The throttle (item 4) is opened one-quarter inch so additional fuel is drawn into the engine cylinders. Then, when the engine starts, it is operating at a low speed which lessens engine wear. Next, the master switch (item 5) is turned on to supply electrical power to the starter motor.

To clear the area, the pilot should open a window or door and shout "Clear" to warn anyone near the airplane that the propeller is about to rotate. The pilot should then listen for a reply and look around to insure that there is no one in the immediate area.

When the pilot is assured that the area is clear, the ignition switch (item 6) is rotated to the start position. When the engine starts, the switch is returned to the both position. It is important to release the starter *as soon as the engine starts* to avoid damage to the starter motor.

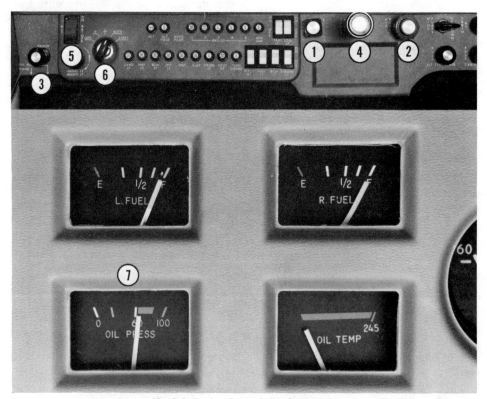

Fig. 2-3. Engine Controls During Starting

When starting an aircraft without a starter, some additional safety considerations are recommended. First, a competent pilot should be at the controls in the cockpit. Second, the person who turns the propeller is in charge. Some of the basic precautions for the person propping the airplane are:

1. Ensure the brakes are set and holding.
2. Always assume the switch is ON.
3. Be sure to stand on firm ground.
4. Never allow any portion of the body to get into the propeller arc.
5. Stand close enough to the propeller to be able to step away easily. (Standing too far away requires leaning forward and increases the possibility of falling into the blades.)
6. When swinging the propeller, move the blade downward with the palms of the hands. (If the blade is moved upward, or gripped tightly with the fingers and a backfire occurs, it could cause broken fingers or the body to be pulled into the blades.)

After the engine is running smoothly, the throttle is adjusted to operate the engine between 800 and 1,000 r.p.m. A low power setting is recommended to prevent undue friction within the engine before the lubricating oil has had a chance to coat the engine's internal parts thoroughly. It is important to check immediately that the oil pressure gauge (item 7) is in the green arc range. If the oil pressure does not register properly within 30 seconds in warm weather or 60 seconds in cold weather, the engine should be shut down to prevent possible damage and to determine the nature of the problem.

SECTION B - TAXIING, ENGINE SHUTDOWN, AND TIEDOWN PROCEDURES

TAXIING

Familiarization with taxiing techniques usually begins on the first training flight. Directional control techniques and proper throttle usage are learned during taxi practice. In addition, the student pilot develops familiarity with control positioning used during crosswind takeoffs and landings later in the training program. In airplanes equipped with tricycle landing gear and a steerable nosewheel, taxiing is relatively easy. However, there are techniques which must be learned and some precautions that should be observed.

USE OF THE THROTTLE

Learning proper use of the throttle begins during taxi operations. In general, good throttle usage is based on smooth, precise adjustments of power. Erratic throttle movement can cause not only directional control difficulties, but can cause the engine to falter.

To aid in proper throttle adjustments, a friction adjustment is incorporated on the throttle assembly. Two types of friction adjustments are shown in figure 2-4. This control can be moved to adjust the friction resistance so the pilot's natural arm movements do not overcontrol the throttle and excessive pressures are not required to advance or close it. In addition, the friction adjustment prevents the throttle from moving because of engine vibration.

POWER CONTROL AND TAXI SPEED

Power control is important for correct taxi techniques. For example, more power is required to *start* the airplane moving than to *keep* it moving. Power should be added slowly until the airplane starts rolling, then reduced to attain the desired taxi speed. In addition, a greater amount of power is required to start and sustain an airplane in motion on a soft surface than on a hard surface.

Taxi speed is controlled primarily with the throttle and secondarily with brakes. The brakes should be used only when a reduction of engine r.p.m. is not sufficient to slow the airplane. The use of high power settings and control of the airplane's direction and speed with brakes causes excessive wear and overheating of the braking system.

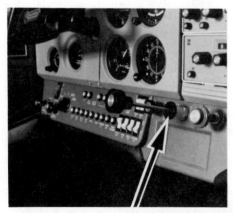

Fig. 2-4. Two Types of Throttle Friction Controls

Light airplanes have brakes on only two wheels and the brakes are relatively small. Therefore, taxi speeds need to be reduced and held within the capability of the braking system. Many flight instructors recommend the use of a taxi speed that is equal to a brisk walk. When operating in confined areas, however, the speed should be slower. A guideline for speeds in confined areas is that if the brakes fail, the airplane can be stopped short of any immediate obstructions by reducing power.

Another useful suggestion for the development of proper taxi speed control is for the pilot to assume that the brakes are inoperative. This helps the pilot learn proper use of power to control taxi speed.

ENGINE COOLING DURING TAXIING

Many aircooled engines are closely baffled and tightly cowled. Because of the slow speeds associated with taxiing and ground operations, only small amounts of cooling air are forced into the engine compartment and over the engine cylinders. Therefore, prolonged ground operations, particularly in warm weather, can cause overheating in the engine cylinders even before the oil temperature gauge indicates a pronounced rise in temperature. If installed, the cylinder head temperature gauge should be used to monitor engine temperature. The airplane manufacturer recommends proper power settings for engine warmup to provide the optimum flow of cooling air through the engine compartment.

DIRECTIONAL CONTROL DURING TAXI

On most airplanes the nosewheel is linked to the rudder pedals and steering is accomplished with rudder pressure. When the right rudder pedal is depressed, the nosewheel turns to the right, causing the airplane to turn right. Conversely, if the left rudder pedal is depressed, the nosewheel turns to the left, causing the airplane to turn left. The angle that the nosewheel can be turned varies with different makes and models of airplanes.

In addition to turning the nosewheel in the direction of the turn, depressing the rudder pedal also causes the rudder to move. Therefore, as illustrated in figure 2-5, airflow over the rudder from taxi

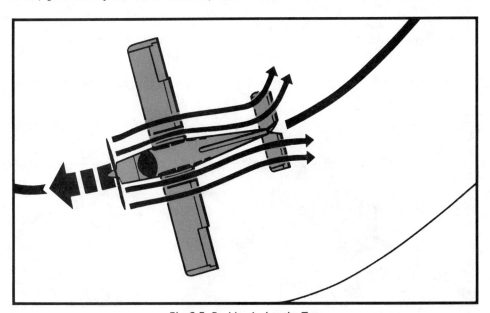

Fig. 2-5. Rudder Assists the Turn

speed, wind, and propeller slipstream provides a small additional force which assists in turning the airplane.

To make a turn of smaller radius than can be accomplished through nosewheel steering alone, the rudder pedal is depressed fully in the direction of turn, followed by light application of the individual toe brake on that rudder pedal. This procedure applies differential braking in the direction of the turn and produces a smaller turn radius. It is possible to make very tight turns by pivoting on one wheel while using heavy differential braking and a large amount of power. However, this is considered poor pilot technique and causes excessive tire wear.

EFFECTS OF WIND ON TAXI TECHNIQUES

Taxiing in calm or light wind conditions at moderate taxi speeds does not require any additional skills or use of other controls. However, when wind speed is moderate or strong, special techniques must be employed. In a strong wind, there is a tendency for the wind to get under the upwind wing and tip the airplane toward the downwind side. This tendency can be counteracted by proper use of flight controls. A study of the necessary control positions for taxiing in

strong wind enables the pilot to compensate for adverse wind effects.

At *slow* speeds the aileron, rudder, and elevator controls are relatively *ineffective*. However, as the speed of air over the controls increases, control effectiveness also increases. There are three factors which affect the speed of the airflow over control surfaces—taxi speed, wind speed, and propeller slipstream. Any one or any combination of the three can act on a control surface at a given time.

The flight controls of the airplane respond the same whether taxiing at five knots in a calm wind or standing still with a five-knot headwind, and the controls are equally effective in both cases. However, if the airplane is taxied at 15 knots *into* a 15-knot wind, the controls have a 30-knot airflow over them and respond to that velocity of airflow.

On the other hand, if the airplane is taxied over the ground at five knots with a *tailwind* of five knots, the taxi speed and the wind speed are canceled and the controls respond as though no wind exists. If the airplane is slowed, the controls respond as though there were an increasing tailwind component. When the airplane is stopped completely, the

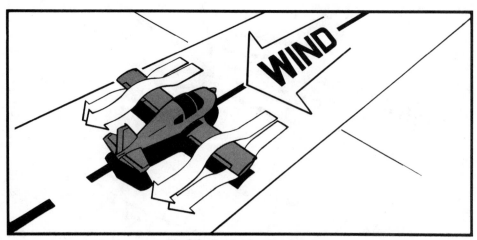

Fig. 2-6. Taxiing in a Headwind

Fig. 2-7. Forward Control Wheel Pressure Increases Weight on Nose Gear

control surfaces are subjected to the direct effects of a five-knot tailwind.

TAXIING IN HEADWINDS

When an airplane is taxied directly into a headwind, the wind flows over and under both wings equally and has no tendency to tip the airplane. (See Fig. 2-6.) Under these conditions, the elevator or stabilator control should be held near neutral or slightly forward of neutral to exert normal pressure on the nose gear.

If the control wheel is held full forward in a strong headwind, the wind striking the downward deflection of the elevator forces the tail section up and the nose down. This condition places more than the normal weight on the nose gear, compresses the nose strut, and brings the propeller tips closer to the ground, as shown in figure 2-7. Normally, this is not hazardous, but on rough terrain this procedure can cause the propeller to be damaged by contact with the ground.

When taxiing over rough ground into a strong headwind, it is recommended that the control wheel be held back, so that the elevator or stabilator is raised. As shown in figure 2-8, this procedure forces the tail down and increases propeller clearance.

Fig. 2-8. Aft Control Wheel Pressure Lightens Weight on Nose Gear

Fig. 2-9. Forward Control Pressure Counteracts Tailwind Overturn Tendency

TAXIING IN TAILWINDS

When taxiing in a strong tailwind, the control wheel should be placed in the full forward position. This causes the wind to strike the upper surface of the elevator or stabilator and exert a downward force on the tail. This procedure prevents the wind from forcing the tail up and causing the airplane to nose over. (See Fig. 2-9.)

TAXIING IN CROSSWINDS

When the wind is blowing from the left or right of the nose, a lifting effect is created on one wing. With the wind blowing against the left side of the nose, as shown in figure 2-10, the wind pushes against the fuselage and, in effect, rolls the airplane to the right. This exposes the lower surface of the left wing to a lifting effect from the wind. The fuselage partially blocks the airflow to the right

wing and a pronounced rolling tendency is produced. Normally, the wind is not strong enough to actually overturn the airplane, but with a strong wind and improper control placement, the airplane could be upset, resulting in damage to the wingtips.

Quartering Headwind

To counteract the tipping tendencies of a left quartering headwind, neutral elevator or stabilator pressure should be applied and the control wheel should be turned full left. Then, the wind flowing over the left wing exerts pressure against the raised aileron, as illustrated in figure 2-11, tending to force that wing down. The airflow under the right wing applies pressure to the lowered aileron and tends to raise the right wing. This combination of forces acts to balance the tipping or rolling effects of the wind.

Fig. 2-10. Effects of Quartering Headwind

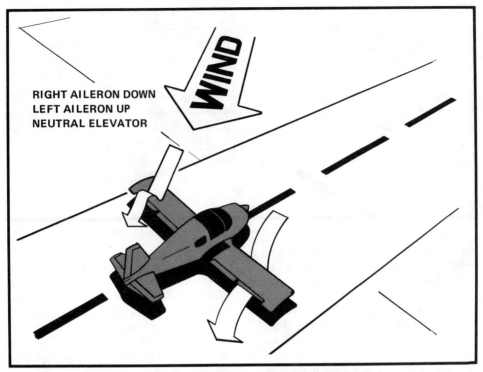

Fig. 2-11. Control Positions for Left Quartering Headwind

When taxiing in quartering wind, the aileron control should be moved to its *full* deflection. This is necessary because at slow taxi speeds, the controls are less effective and a small amount of deflection may be of little value.

As wind velocity increases, the tipping tendency becomes more pronounced. However, with a strong wind, the ailerons are more effective, which tends to compensate for this effect. With a quartering headwind, the elevator is used in the same manner as when taxiing directly into a headwind.

When the wind is quartering from ahead and the right, the tipping tendency is to the left, as shown in figure 2-12. In this

Fig. 2-12. Control Positions for Right Quartering Headwind

Fig. 2-13. Control Positions for Left Quartering Tailwind

situation, the control wheel is turned full right so the right aileron is raised and the left aileron is lowered. In this position, the ailerons provide a restoring force to counteract the tipping force and the elevator can be used as if taxiing straight into the wind.

Taxiing with a quartering headwind is exactly the same condition encountered in a crosswind takeoff or landing. An understanding of the effects of wind and the development of the technique and feel for the airplane in a quartering headwind can be applied directly to future takeoff and landing practice.

Quartering Tailwind

When the wind is striking an airplane from behind, the ailerons must be positioned to counteract the tipping tendency and the control wheel must be rotated *away* from the wind. When the wind is from the left rear, referred to as a left quartering tailwind, the aileron control must be turned to the right, as shown in figure 2-13. This results in a downward aerodynamic force on the lowered left aileron and an upward force on the right aileron. The effects of strong quartering tailwinds on high-wing, nosewheel-equipped airplanes can be critical. Therefore, caution is recommended. Pilots also should avoid sudden bursts of the throttle and abrupt braking.

Since quartering tailwinds also have a tendency to flow beneath the elevator or stabilator and lift the tail, the airplane may tip over on the nosewheel and one main wheel. To counteract this tipping force, the elevator control is moved forward so the elevator is lowered. The tailwind then applies an aerodynamic force on the top of the elevator and tends to push the tail down.

The pilot must be particularly cautious when slowing down and beginning a turn in a quartering tailwind. As shown in figure 2-14, the increasing tailwind component combined with the normal tendency of the airplane to tip during the turn, makes the airplane especially vulnerable to being overturned. Slow taxi speeds and slow turns minimize this danger.

During much of the time that the pilot spends taxiing, the winds will probably be at a level where control positioning is not critical. However, he should realize that determination of wind direction with respect to the airplane heading and use of proper control placement require practice.

PRACTICING PROPER CONTROL POSITIONING

Proper control positioning should be practiced on every flight. When there are light winds, it should be assumed that the winds are strong and from whichever

Fig. 2-14. Turning with a Tailwind Requires Caution

direction the windsock indicates. Then, correct placement of the aileron and elevator or stabilator controls can be conscientiously practiced as if they were necessary.

The benefits of this practice will be evident later in the flight training program when the student actually encounters strong winds. In addition, he will develop a constant awareness of wind direction early in the program. By the time the airplane has reached the takeoff position on any given flight, the pilot will have evaluated wind speed and direction. He will be able to determine what crosswind takeoff and landing techniques are required before reaching the runup area.

HAND SIGNALS

Instruction in taxiing should include familiarization with the standard hand signals used by ramp attendants for directing pilots during ground operations. Figure 2-15 illustrates these sig-

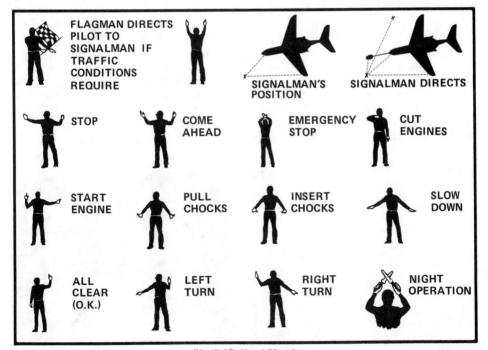

Fig. 2-15. Hand Signals

nals. The beginning pilot should study these signals carefully prior to his first instructional flight and review them periodically during the first few hours of training.

ENGINE SHUTDOWN AND PARKING PROCEDURES

At completion of a flight, the airplane should be taxied into the parking area utilizing a safe taxi speed and proper control procedures. After reaching the desired parking area, the pilot should proceed with the engine shutdown according to the checklist. A typical checklist is shown in figure 2-16.

MOVING THE AIRPLANE USING A TOWBAR

Most light tricycle-gear airplanes are safely and easily maneuvered by using a towbar attached to the nosewheel. The towbar normally is stowed in the baggage compartment and should be used when available. The fixed-base operator usually has an assortment of towbars for use if one is not available in the airplane.

When using a towbar, it is necessary to insure that the nose gear is not turned beyond its steering radius limits. (See Fig. 2-17.) There are limit stops on some airplanes which restrict the gear from turning beyond a given arc. Others have

limit marks painted on the gear to indicate the travel range permitted. Turning the nose gear in either direction beyond its steering radius limits can result in damage to the nose gear and steering mechanism.

MOVING THE AIRPLANE WITHOUT A TOWBAR

Since the structure of an airplane is composed of lightweight materials, certain points must be used for pushing or pulling the airplane. If a towbar is not available, the following procedures should be used.

PIVOTING THE AIRPLANE

A tricycle-gear airplane can be pivoted about one main wheel if the nose gear is lifted off of the ground by applying downward pressure on the tail section. However, care must be exercised where pressure is applied. Pressure should be applied over a bulkhead just ahead of the vertical fin, as shown in figure 2-18, part A. The tail of an airplane can be depressed by applying hand pressure on the front spar, close to the fuselage (part B). Pressure should not be applied to the outer ends of the horizontal stabilizer or elevator or to the stabilator. With the tail depressed, the nosewheel will clear the ground and the airplane can be turned readily in either direction by pivoting it on one of the main wheels (part C).

```
1. Parking Brakes — SET
2. Electrical and Radio Equipment — OFF
3. Flaps — UP
4. Propeller— HIGH RPM
5. Throttle — CLOSE
6. Mixture — IDLE CUT OFF
7. Magneto/Start Switch — OFF, after engine stops
8. Master Switch — OFF
9. Alternator Switch — OFF
10. Control Lock — INSTALL
11. Wheel Chocks — INSTALL
12. Park Brake — RELEASE, if airplane is
    left unattended
```

Fig. 2-16. Engine Shutdown Checklist

Fig. 2-17. Nosewheel Turning Limits

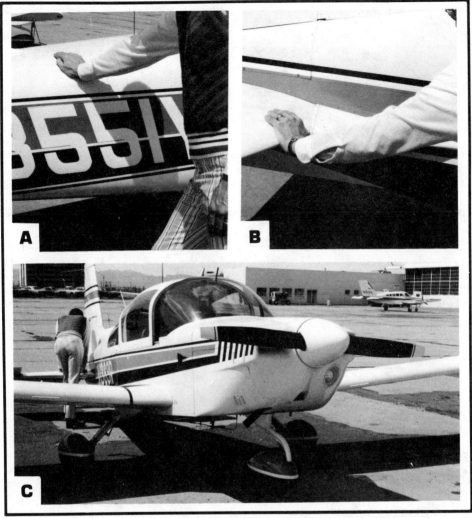

Fig. 2-18. Pivoting a Tricycle-Gear Airplane by Hand

The wingtips of the airplane should be observed carefully because one wingtip moves aft while the other moves forward. Structural damage can result if a wingtip strikes another object.

Pivoting a tailwheel-type airplane is quite easy because the tailwheel usually pivots 360°. One person can turn the airplane around by pushing on the side of the fuselage over a bulkhead, adjacent to the horizontal stabilizer, as shown in figure 2-19.

Fig. 2-19. Pivoting a Tailwheel Airplane by Hand

Fig. 2-20. Push at Stabilizer Rib Locations

PUSHING THE AIRPLANE

Pushing on the leading edge of the horizontal stabilizer is acceptable if cau-

tion is exercised. Pressure should be applied only at rib locations near the fuselage, as shown in figure 2-20, and up or down loads should be avoided.

The leading edge of the wing is also a good push point on low wing airplanes. Again, pressure must be applied only at rib locations. When the wing is used as a push point, more than one person is needed to maintain directional control of the airplane. On high wing airplanes, wing struts make good push points, as shown in figure 2-21, but two persons are required to move the airplane easily.

The propeller should not be pushed or pulled. If pressure is applied to the propeller tip, it may be permanently bent and produce a serious vibration problem in flight. If pushing on the propeller is necessary, it should be done *near the hub*. The nosecap of the engine

Fig. 2-21. Wing Struts Provide Good Push Points

cowling and the trailing edges of wings and control surfaces are not designed for the type of load incurred and should not be used to move the airplane.

SECURING THE AIRPLANE

Proper tiedown procedures are the best precaution against damage to a parked airplane by strong or gusty winds. When the airplane is in the proper tiedown area, chocks should be placed in front of and behind the main wheels and the parking brake released (if set).

CONTROL LOCK INSTALLATION

All flight controls should be secured to prevent the control surfaces from striking the stops. Most airplanes are equipped with internal control locks operable from the cockpit, while on others, it may be necessary to use external padded battens (control surface locks). Even if the airplane is equipped with internal control locks, the additional use of external locks may be necessary to prevent gust loads from being fed back into the control system during extremely strong or gusty wind conditions.

When using external control locks, streamers or lines to the tiedown anchors should be fastened to the locks. This provides a means of alerting the pilot and airport ramp personnel to remove the external locks prior to flight.

WING AND TAIL TIEDOWN

The wing tiedown should be accomplished with nylon or Dacron tiedown ropes or chains capable of resisting a pull of approximately 3,000 pounds. They should be secured without slack, but should not be tight. Too much slack allows the airplane to jerk against the ropes, while too little slack may permit high stresses to be placed on the airplane. Tiedown ropes actually can put inverted flight stresses on the airplane and many are not designed to take excessive inverted loads.

The tail tiedown should be taut but not so tight it raises the nose of the airplane. In a headwind situation, a raised nose increases the angle of attack of the wing and creates additional lifting force, causing more pressure on the wing tiedown restraints.

Figure 2-22 shows the proper method for securing an airplane using a chain tiedown. One link on the free end of the chain is passed through a link of the taut portion and a safety snap is used to keep the link from passing back through. Therefore, any load on the chain is borne by the chain itself instead of the snap.

A mass tiedown arrangement used by many airport operators consists of continuous links of parallel wire ropes passed through U-bolt anchors, secured in cement within the ramp surface. Tiedown chains are attached to the wire rope with roundpin anchor shackles. This allows the tiedown chains to move along the wire rope and provide a variable distance between anchor points so a variety of large, medium, and small airplanes can use the vertical tiedowns

Fig. 2-22. Use of a Chain Tiedown

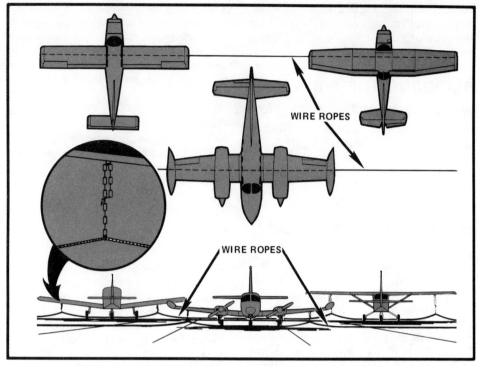

Fig. 2-23. Typical Airplane Tiedown System

without loss of space. Top and front views of a typical wire rope tiedown system are shown in figure 2-23.

CLEANUP

After the aircraft is secured, the pilot should make a careful check of the interior of the airplane. All switches must be off and trash, papers, or flight planning items should be cleaned from the cabin area. On the exterior of the airplane, the pitot tube cover should be installed if applicable and the propeller placed in a horizontal position to lessen the possibility of damage caused by another taxiing aircraft's wingtip. Placement of the propeller in a horizontal position also permits the spinner to offer more protection to the prop hub from rain, snow, and ice. This is especially important of an aircraft equipped with a constant speed propeller.

SECTION C - TRAFFIC PATTERNS

A normal traffic pattern is rectangular and has five named legs and a designated altitude, as shown in figure 2-24. This type of pattern normally is used at airports not served by control towers. Since all turns are to the left, this pattern is called a left-hand pattern. The pilot will find variations from the described pattern at different localities and at airports with control towers. For example, a right-hand pattern, as shown in figure 2-25, may be designated to expedite the flow of traffic when obstacles or concentrations of population make the use of a left-hand pattern undesirable.

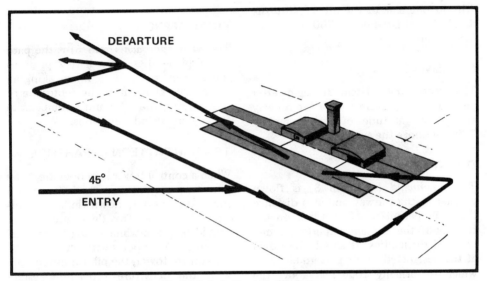

Fig. 2-24. Left-Hand Traffic Pattern

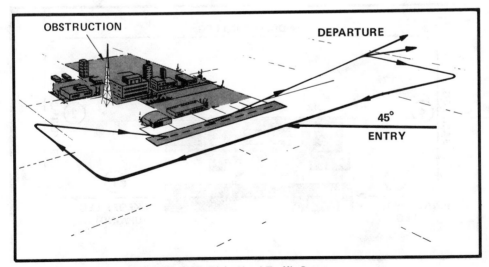

Fig. 2-25. Right-Hand Traffic Pattern

TRAFFIC PATTERN LEGS

TAKEOFF LEG

The *takeoff leg*, as shown in figure 2-26, item 1, normally consists of the airplane's flight path after takeoff, up to the initial altitude of approximately 700 feet AGL. This leg also is called the *upwind leg*. The airplane is flown directly above an imaginary extension of the runway centerline and not permitted to drift to one side or the other. No turns should be initiated below 700 feet above the surface.

CROSSWIND LEG

The *crosswind leg* (item 2) begins after passing the departure end of the runway and at an altitude of approximately 700 feet above the surface.

DOWNWIND LEG

The *downwind leg* (item 3) is flown parallel to the runway and at a distance that will permit a safe landing on the runway if the airplane experiences mechanical difficulties. It should be flown at the designated traffic pattern altitude, which is normally 1000 feet above the ground.

BASE LEG

The *base leg* (item 4) begins at a point selected according to other traffic and wind conditions. If the wind is very strong, the turn begins sooner than normal. If the wind is light, the turn to base is delayed. Small errors in the downwind leg due to misjudgment in speed, height, and distance from the runway can be compensated for by adjusting the turn to base leg.

FINAL APPROACH

The *final approach* (item 5) is the path the airplane flies immediately prior to touchdown. Since it is flown along an imaginary extension of the centerline of the runway, the pilot must compensate for any crosswind conditions.

TRAFFIC PATTERN DEPARTURE

When a control tower is in operation, the pilot can request and receive approval for a straight-out, downwind, or right-hand departure. This departure request should be made while asking for takeoff clearance. At airports without an operating control tower, the pilot must comply with the departure procedures established for that airport. These procedures

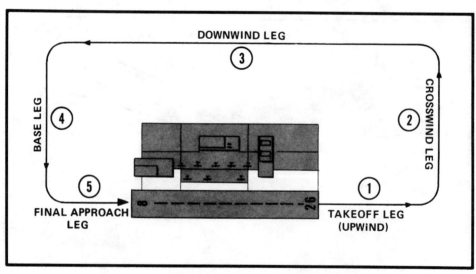

Fig. 2-26. Traffic Pattern Legs

usually are posted by airport operators so pilots can become familiar with the local rules.

TRAFFIC PATTERN ENTRY

Traffic pattern entry procedures at airports with an operating control tower are specified by the tower operator. At uncontrolled airports, traffic pattern altitudes and entry procedures may vary according to established local procedures. This pattern is usually entered at a 45° angle to the downwind leg, abeam the midpoint of the runway. Airport advisory service or UNICOM should be utilized when available, for receipt of traffic pattern and landing information.

The pilot should also broadcast his intentions over the appropriate frequency when taking off or landing at an uncontrolled airport. The *Airman's Information Manual* provides a complete listing of the proper frequencies to use in various situations. The following list provides a condensed version of the AIM data.

1. No tower or FSS —Communicate with the UNICOM operator, or if unable to contact the operator, use the appropriate UNICOM frequency to broadcast position or intentions in the blind.
2. Part-time tower closed, FSS closed —Broadcast position or intentions in the blind on tower frequency.

3. FSS closed — no tower — Broadcast position or intentions in the blind on 123.6 MHz.
4. No tower, FSS, or UNICOM operator —Broadcast position or intentions in the blind on 122.9 MHz.

5. Part-time tower closed, FSS open —Communicate with FSS on tower frequency for airport information. At non-FAA tower locations, use 123.6 MHz.

TRAFFIC PATTERN COURTESIES

Occasionally, a number of airplanes may be in the traffic pattern practicing landings and takeoffs. If they all assume normal spacing, they may completely block the pattern. Other airplanes attempting to enter the pattern or take off from the airport will have difficulty acquiring a safe spacing. If a pilot in the pattern sees another pilot attempting to take off or land, he should extend his traffic pattern and allow the airplane room for a proper entry.

COLLISION AVOIDANCE

The primary responsibility for collision avoidance rests with the pilot. Although several systems have been designed as safety aids, nothing can replace pilot vigilance. Airport operations require constant effort to see and avoid other aircraft. The pilot should make a point of checking both the approach and departure paths prior to takeoff or landing. This procedure should be followed at *both* controlled and uncontrolled airports. The use of anti-collision and landing lights during final approach or climbout will make an aircraft more clearly visible. During climbout, the airplane may be accelerated to cruise climb speed as soon as a safe altitude is reached, since the higher speed will result in a lower pitch attitude and increased forward visibility. In addition, turns of more than 90° should be avoided while in the traffic pattern. If a 360° turn is required for proper spacing, it should be interrupted as necessary to clear the airspace ahead of the aircraft.

During all operations, the pilot must maintain an awareness of blind spots which are inherent in aircraft design. Clearing turns should be employed to expose the airspace which has been hidden by the aircraft nose and wings. Prior to flight maneuvers, the pilot should perform two 90° clearing turns; before beginning a turn, he must pay special attention to the airspace in the direction of the turn as well as the airspace which will become blocked by the aircraft structure after the turn is established. Figure 2-27 illustrates the airspace not visible to the pilot as a result of airplane design.

In order to see something clearly under normal illumination, an individual must look directly at the object. Studies have shown that the eye perceives poorly if an image is moving across the retina of the eye. When scanning for other aircraft, the scan should be acomplished by sectors, rather than permitting the eyes to sweep across the sky. Each successive sector of the sky is brought into focus separately, providing the sharpest images for the eye to discern. Visual scanning involves a systematic search of the entire visual field through use of both eye and head movements.

The pilot should utilize such voluntary programs as airport advisory service and radar traffic advisories, when available. Not only does participation aid the pilot in detecting otherwise unobserved traffic, but it also makes his positions and intentions known.

The pilot must be aware that the provision of radar traffic advisory service by ATC does not always include separation from other traffic. Separation is provided to VFR aircraft *only* when participating in Stage III radar service or operating in a terminal control area. It must also be remembered that, at no time is the pilot relieved of the responsibility of seeing and avoiding other traffic.

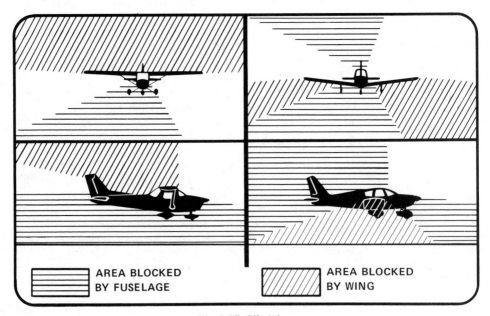

AREA BLOCKED BY FUSELAGE

AREA BLOCKED BY WING

Fig. 2-27. Blind Areas

chapter 3

GROUND REFERENCE MANEUVERS

INTRODUCTION

Early in the flight training program, maneuvers are practiced well above traffic pattern altitude. The primary purpose for this practice is to help the pilot learn how the airplane feels and responds in various configurations and flight conditions and to develop his ability to control the airplane with smoothness and precision.

When the pilot can maintain elementary control of the airplane, he begins to practice problems that require him to divide his attention between flying the airplane and following prescribed paths over the ground. In addition, the maneuvers prepare the pilot for maneuvering in the traffic pattern and making approaches, landings, and departures where a division of attention within and outside of the airplane is required for the safe conduct of flight.

If local terrain conditions permit, these *ground reference maneuvers* can be practiced initially at approximately 600 feet above ground level. At this altitude, the effects of wind are readily apparent. As proficiency increases, however, the turns must be conducted at traffic pattern altitude. Simple ground reference maneuvers are taught early in the program and, as the pilot gains experience, more complex maneuvers place additional demands on his planning, timing, coordination, and smooth control of the airplane.

SECTION A - TRACKING A STRAIGHT LINE AND CONSTANT RADIUS TURNS

A basic requirement for performance of any ground reference maneuver is the ability to fly a straight line between two points, as shown in figure 3-1. In a no-wind condition, the pilot can select a position on the ground and fly directly to that point. However, if the airplane is controlled in the same manner in a cross-wind, the airplane will drift to one side.

TERMINOLOGY

Before performing ground reference maneuvers, the pilot should understand three terms. *Heading* pertains to the airplane's magnetic heading, while *track* refers to the path of the airplane over the ground. *Crab* or wind correction angle, indicates a turn into the wind to correct for drift.

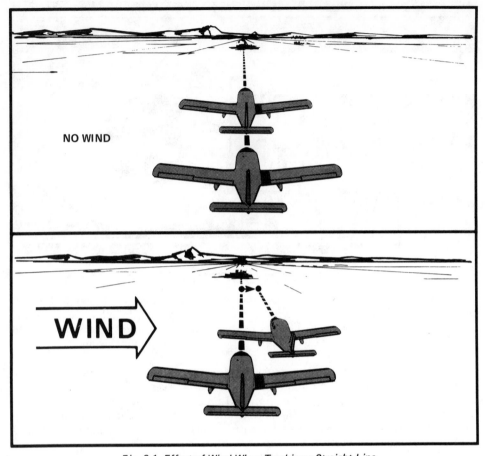

Fig. 3-1. Effect of Wind When Tracking a Straight Line

WIND DRIFT CORRECTION TECHNIQUES

If the pilot simply adjusts the airplane heading periodically to aim at a point, the ground track assumes a curved shape until the airplane is headed into the wind, as shown in figure 3-2. The accepted method for correcting the effects of wind is to make a coordinated turn into the wind so the nose of the airplane no longer points toward the intended point on the ground. Instead, it is turned in the direction from which the wind is blowing. The magnitude of this coordinated turn is determined by wind speed and direction. This crabbing technique gives the appearance that the airplane is flying sideways, as shown in figure 3-3. However, this is an illusion, since the

airplane is still flying directly into the oncoming airstream (relative wind) just as in a calm wind situation.

When solving cross-country navigation problems, the pilot computes the course between any two points, then obtains a forecast of wind direction and speed. These known quantities and the true airspeed can be set on a flight computer and a specific heading and wind correction angle can be computed. However, for ground reference maneuvers, the amount of wind correction is determined by the trial-and-error method. That is, the airplane is established on a heading and drift is observed, as shown by figure 3-4, positions 1 and 2. Then, as illustrated at position 2, the pilot turns the airplane to compensate for drift, holds

Fig. 3-2. Incorrect Wind Drift Correction Technique

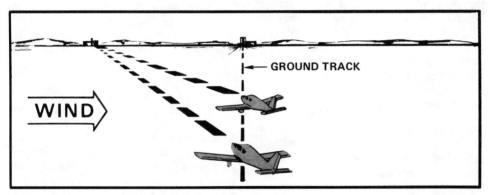

Fig. 3-3. Crab Correction for Wind Drift

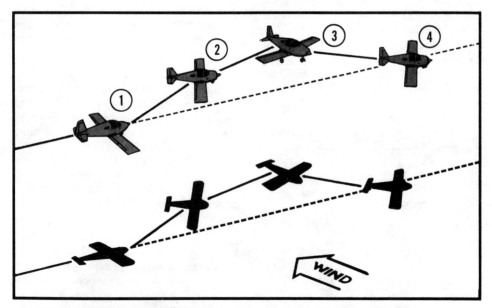

Fig. 3-4. Trial-And-Error Method Used to Establish Correct Crab

that new heading, and observes the new ground track, as diagrammed between positions 2 and 3. If the airplane is still drifting from the desired track, the pilot should make another heading correction, as shown at position 3, hold this heading, observe the track, and continue this process through a series of small corrections until he has arrived at the heading necessary to maintain the desired track.

COORDINATION

All turns made while performing ground reference maneuvers should be coordinated turns. Aileron, rudder, and elevator pressures are applied as in earlier practice. There should be no tendency to skid the nose with the rudder in order to change the heading slightly and the pilot should not attempt to hold a crab angle with rudder pressure.

DETERMINING DRIFT

To determine the amount of drift, a point on the ground is aligned with a reference point in line with the pilot's eyes. As illustrated in figure 3-5, this imaginary line of sight passes from the pilot's eyes, through the windshield, and intercepts the horizon. If there is no drift, the point on the ground and the reference point stay in alignment as the airplane proceeds toward the point on the ground. On the other hand, if the airplane is drifting, the reference line drifts downwind from the point on the ground.

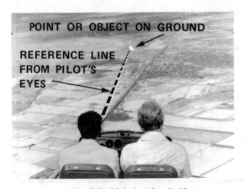

Fig. 3-5. Sighting for Drift

To establish the proper drift correction angle, the reference line of sight must be moved to the downwind side of the point on the ground over which the intended track must pass. As the airplane continues toward the ground point, the crab angle tends to give the appearance that the airplane is sliding along sideways. In fact, the airplane is moving sideways in reference to the ground. When the pilot has applied the right amount of drift correction, the angle between his reference line of sight and the point over which he intends to pass remains fixed.

The ability to hold a constant heading is important in maintaining a successful track. If the pilot's normal variations in heading control are excessive, he will not be able to maintain his desired course over the ground.

The pilot can prepare for flying ground reference maneuvers by determining the direction of the wind before he leaves the airport and verifying the direction and velocity as he approaches the practice area. The runway in use, windsock indication, and movement of smoke are valuable clues. (See Fig. 3-6.) Wind also produces advancing wave patterns on water and grain fields and leans rows of trees away from the wind.

By the time a road or an imaginary line between two points is selected for practice in tracking a straight line between two points, the pilot should have the direction and speed of the wind in mind so he can make an initial estimate of the crab angle required. Coordinated turns are used to make small corrections to the initial crab angle. The track over the ground reveals if the student has the proper drift correction angle established.

While performing these basic tracking problems, the pilot also gains some feel for the airplane's speed over the ground. The ability to recognize ground-speed changes is important, because it

Fig. 3-6. Useful Clues to Wind Direction and Velocity

helps the pilot anticipate and plan his flight path in order to perform precise ground reference maneuvers.

The explanation and guidelines given can be very helpful in understanding the theory of drift correction necessary to fly precise ground reference maneuvers. Once the pilot actually observes these effects in the airplane, the tracking procedure becomes very simple.

CONSTANT RADIUS TURNS

The effects of wind on a turning airplane are not quite so obvious as on an airplane in straight flight. Figure 3-7 illustrates that if an airplane turns at a constant angle of bank in a calm wind condition, the track over the ground is circular and the airplane completes the turn over the point where it began.

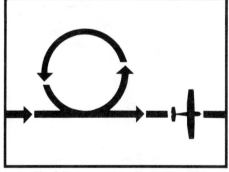

Fig. 3-7. Ground Track With Constant Bank (No Wind)

A turn performed at a constant angle of bank in a headwind, however, produces an oval ground track. The turn is completed on the original track, but behind the point where it started. The distorted ground track is shown on the left in figure 3-8. This type of turn performed in a direct crosswind also produces a distorted ground track. The turn is com-

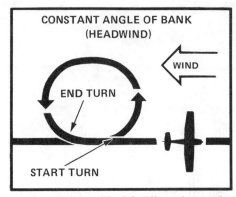
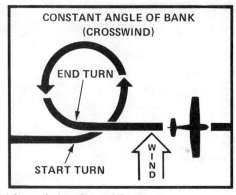

Fig. 3-8. Effect of Headwind and Crosswind on Ground Track

pleted abreast of, but on the downwind side of the point where it started, as illustrated in the right portion of figure 3-8.

To perform a constant radius turn in a wind, the angle of bank must be varied to change the rate of turn. The steepest bank is at the point of greatest groundspeed. The steeper bank and higher rate of turn are required to turn the airplane faster, since its speed over the ground

has increased. This point of greatest groundspeed exists when the airplane is flying directly downwind and the true airspeed plus the wind speed result in the higher groundspeed. These relationships are shown in figure 3-9.

In contrast, the shallowest angle of bank is at the point of slowest groundspeed. The shallower bank and slower rate of turn are necessary because the airplane is passing over the ground more slowly. As

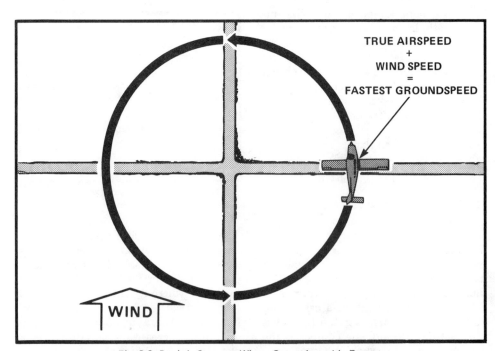

Fig. 3-9. Bank Is Steepest Where Groundspeed Is Fastest

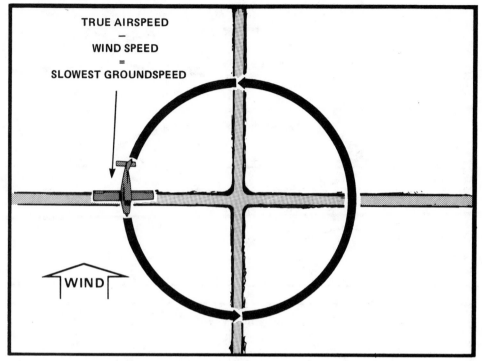

TRUE AIRSPEED
—
WIND SPEED
=
SLOWEST GROUNDSPEED

WIND

Fig. 3-10. Shallowest Angle of Bank Is at Point of Slowest Groundspeed

shown in figure 3-10, the point of slowest groundspeed occurs when the airplane is going directly into the wind. At this point, the true airspeed minus the wind speed results in a slower groundspeed.

The groundspeed is the same for the portions of the turn performed in a direct crosswind, since the crosswind adds neither a headwind nor a tailwind component to affect the groundspeed. Groundspeed at these points is an average of the speeds on the downwind and upwind portions. Therefore, the angle of bank is a value midway between the steep downwind bank and the shallow upwind bank, as shown in figure 3-11.

To make a turn that traces a perfect circle over the ground, the angle of bank must be changed constantly throughout the entire circular maneuver, as seen in

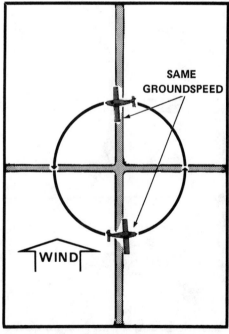

SAME GROUNDSPEED

WIND

Fig. 3-11. Same Angle of Bank Required on Up-wind and Downwind Sides of Turn

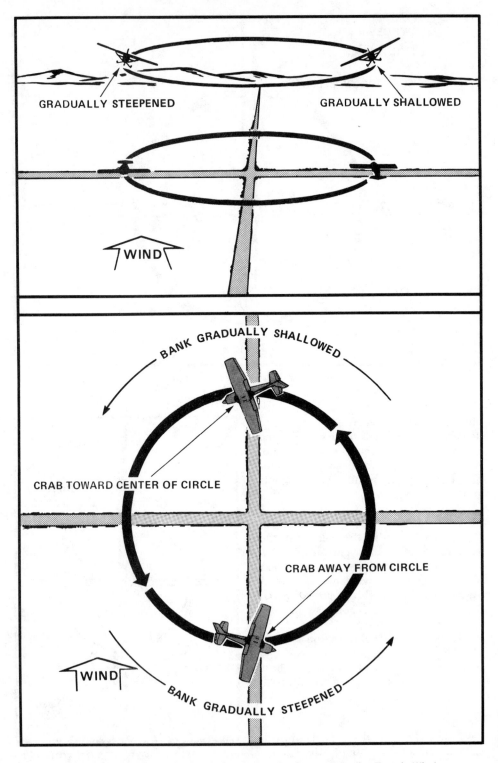

Fig. 3-12. Bank Angle and Crab Corrections for Constant Radius Turn in Wind

the top portion of figure 3-12. The bank is steepened gradually from its shallowest point until the steepest bank is achieved when the airplane is flying directly downwind. From this point, the bank is gradually shallowed. Throughout the maneuver, the pilot must learn to anticipate the bank angle changes.

As with any maneuver, proper wind drift techniques must be applied during constant radius turns. On the downwind side of the turn, the nose must be crabbed toward the center of the circle, as illustrated in the bottom portion of figure 3-12 On the upwind side, it must be crabbed away from the center of the circle.

As the pilot looks out his side window on the upwind side of the circle, the center of the circle appears behind the lateral axis of the airplane, which usually is located near the front spar of the wing. In contrast, as the pilot looks out the side window on the downwind side, the center of the circle appears to be ahead of the lateral axis. This relationship is most pronounced when the airplane is directly crosswind. As the airplane flies directly upwind or downwind, the lateral axis appears to be nearly aligned with the center of the circle.

SECTION B-RECTANGULAR COURSES AND ELEMENTARY EIGHTS

Rectangular courses and elementary eights provide practice in the methods used to track over the ground and to evaluate the crab angle. Important objectives are to learn the division of attention required to maintain the flight path, observe ground reference points, look for other traffic, and maintain altitude.

RECTANGULAR COURSES

The instructor normally selects a field well away from other traffic where the sides are not more than a mile or less than one-half mile in length. These dimensions are rough guidelines, but the shape should be square or rectangular within the approximate limits given. The maneuver is initially flown at approximately 600 feet. During later traffic pattern practice, it is flown at the appropriate traffic pattern altitude. The bank angle in the turning portions of the pattern should not exceed the medium bank recommended for flight in the traffic pattern.

This maneuver requires the pilot to combine several flight techniques. First, he may need to use varying crab angles throughout the course. Second, he must track an imaginary line parallel to a fixed line. Third, he must plan ahead and use different angles of bank in order to roll out of the turns at the proper distance from the field boundary. Each turn should be comprised of approximately one-fourth of a constant radius turn, as shown in figure 3-13.

The flight path should not be directly over the edges of the field, but far enough away that the boundaries can be observed as the pilot looks out the side windows of the airplane. If an attempt is made to fly over the edge of the field, the required turns will be too steep or the maneuver will result in an oval-shaped course. The closer the track of the airplane is to the edges of the field, the steeper the bank required. The determining factor in selecting the distance from the field boundary should be the

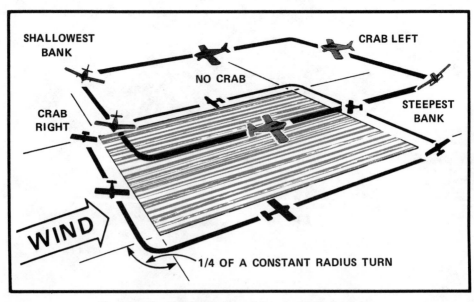

Fig. 3-13. Rectangular Course and Required Drift Corrections

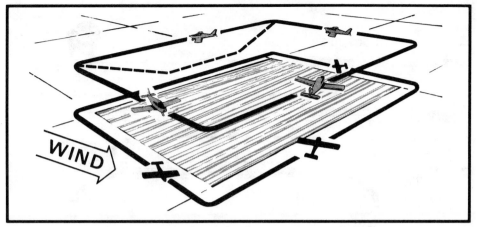

Fig. 3-14. Wind Blowing Diagonally Across Rectangular Course

normal distance from the runway of the downwind leg of a typical airport traffic pattern.

When the proper position has been determined, the airplane is flown parallel to one side of the field until the corner is approached. A turn is started at the exact time the airplane is abeam the corner. In this way a ground track parallel to and equidistant from the next side of the field is achieved upon recovery from the turn. This process is repeated at each corner and continued around the field for several trips. If the instructor specifies a certain number of circuits, it is the student's responsibility to count them and stop when the required number has been completed. After several circuits of the field, the direction of the flight path can be reversed.

While flying rectangular courses, the student may be requested to alternately glide on the simulated final approach leg and climb back to the simulated traffic pattern altitude. This provides more realistic practice in approach and climb-out from an airport. The complexity of the maneuver is increased when a wind blows across the rectangular course diagonally, as shown in figure 3-14. In this situation, a crab must be used on all four legs. Practice is devoted to these exer-

cises until proficiency is shown in all phases, correct ground tracks are flown at the specified altitudes, and any traces of tension and confusion are eliminated.

ACCEPTABLE PERFORMANCE FOR RECTANGULAR COURSES

The pilot must readily select the ground reference and maintain the desired track in relation to that reference. Coordinated turns, smooth control usage, and proper division of attention are required. Deviation of 100 feet from the selected altitude is considered disqualifying unless corrected promptly. Excessive maneuvering to correct for wind drift, flight below the minimum safe altitude prescribed by regulations, or inadequate clearance from other aircraft also is disqualifying.

ELEMENTARY EIGHTS

Practice in flying elementary eights often begins with eights along a road. Although this maneuver may be flown with the wind blowing across or parallel to the road, for simplification, only the latter is explained. The principles are common in either case.

To perform eights along a road, the student flies downwind above the road to a predetermined point, such as a fence row or intersection of another road. At this point, the student initiates a 180° turn using a

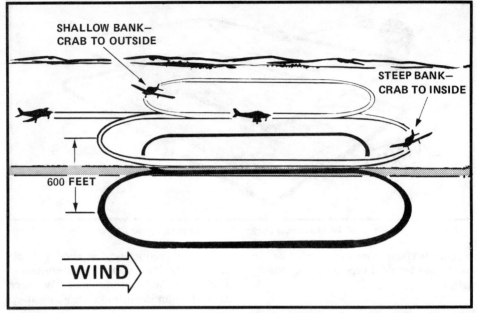

SHALLOW BANK—
CRAB TO OUTSIDE

STEEP BANK—
CRAB TO INSIDE

600 FEET

WIND

Fig. 3-15. Eights Along a Road

medium bank and varying bank angle to trace a half circle ground track. (See Fig. 3-15.)

He then flies upwind along the road, remaining approximately the same distance from the road as when flying the rectangular course. The length of the straight flight portion can vary from one-half mile to more than one mile.

After the straight flight portion, another 180° turn is made over a fenceline or road. This turn also should result in a half circle ground track and the roll-out should place the airplane back over the road again. Then, the second downwind leg is flown and the other half of the eight is performed on the opposite side of the road.

During the segment of the eight in which the pilot is turning downwind, relatively steeper banks are required; however, shallower banks are necessary to counteract the effect of wind drift on the segments in which he is turning upwind. This principle usually is well established in the pilot's mind from previous practice

of rectangular courses. Eights along a road are practiced in both directions until the proper compensation for wind in terms of changing bank angle and crab to maintain the desired ground track is learned.

EIGHTS ACROSS A ROAD

Eights across a road or through an intersection serve as a foundation for performance of eights around pylons. The basic principle of correcting for drift by varying the angle of bank, rate of turn, and crab angle is required to fly this maneuver.

Eights across a road combine both turns and straight flight in order to maintain a preplanned path over the ground. The maneuver usually is performed at the intersection of two roads and, if possible, is flown when a moderate wind exists. The objective is to fly equal-sized loops on each side of the intersection. This requires careful planning because bank varies from steep to shallow and back to steep again, as illustrated in figure 3-16.

The four straight legs should be flown with the wings level, and the track should cross the intersection of the roads at the same angle each time. Determining the proper time to roll into and out of banks helps the pilot establish the proper crab angle and assists him in determining the length of the straight legs. These skills, plus varying the angle of bank to correct for wind drift, further sharpen planning skills and the ability to maneuver the airplane precisely.

As a pilot becomes more proficient in flying the maneuver, he may be asked to perform the eights by rolling from one bank directly into the next while directly over the intersection. This increases the necessity for careful planning.

ACCEPTABLE PERFORMANCE FOR EIGHTS ALONG OR ACROSS A ROAD

The pilot must maneuver the airplane so the loops of the eight are symmetrical. Performance is evaluated on the basis of proper wind drift correction, airspeed control, coordination, altitude control, and vigilance for other aircraft. Deviation of 100 feet from the selected altitude is considered disqualifying unless corrected promptly. Excessively steep banks, flight below the minimum safe altitude prescribed by regulations, or inadequate clearance of other aircraft also is disqualifying.

EIGHTS AROUND PYLONS

Eights around pylons are similar to eights across a road except the loops are made around two prominent points on the ground. The entry to this maneuver should be made downwind and perpendicular to a line drawn between the two points, as illustrated in the top portion of figure 3-17. The entry is made in a manner similar to that used for turns around a point. Both the distance of the point of entry from the pylon and the wind velocity determine the initial angle of bank required to maintain a constant radius from the pylon during each loop. The airspeed should be set at normal cruise speed and the angle of bank should not exceed 45°.

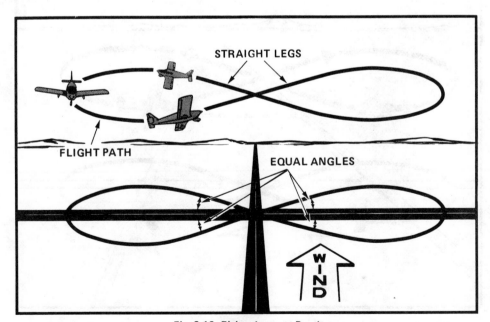

Fig. 3-16. Eights Across a Road

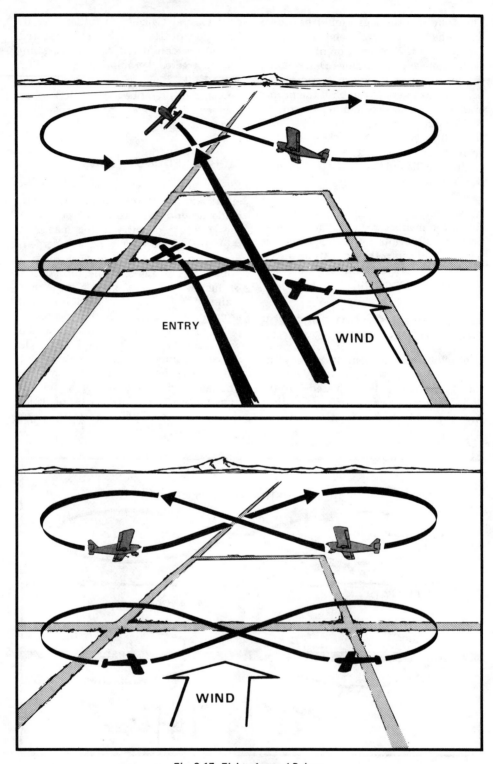

ENTRY

WIND

WIND

Fig. 3-17. Eights Around Pylons

As illustrated in the lower portion of figure 3-17, the loops are made at a constant radius and both loops are equal in size. The pylons should be selected and the turns planned so there is approximately three to five seconds of straight flight between the loops.

This maneuver is a combination of two fundamental flight maneuvers—turns and straight-and-level flight. Since the objective of the turning portions of eights around pylons is to maintain a constant radius from the pylon, this part of the maneuver closely resembles a turn about a point, except that a complete circle is not made.

BANK ANGLE

The bank angle changes continuously throughout the turn in windy conditions. The amount of bank variation depends on the wind velocity. Bank should be gradually decreased from the steepest bank at turn entry to the shallowest bank as the airplane heads directly into the wind on the outer edges of the eight. From these points, a gradual increase in bank takes place until the steepest bank is reached again just prior to roll-out for the straight flight segments. Roll-out from the turns should be completed on a heading that insures that flight during the straight-and-level segment will carry the airplane to the turn entry point for the second pylon.

As the pilot gains experience in flying eights around pylons, he may be encouraged to start the maneuver at any point in order to save flying time and to improve his judgment and orientation. However, he should be sure that the airplane is positioned to fly downwind between the pylons, as shown in the upper portion of figure 3-17.

DRIFT CORRECTION

In a wind, the principles of drift correction must be employed to maintain the proper ground track around the pylon. Roll-out from one loop may have to be made with the airplane headed toward some point on the upwind side of the next pylon. The exact heading is determined by trial and error. As a point from "which to work," the roll-out from each loop should be made with the airplane headed toward the other pylon. An estimate of the amount of increase or decrease in the crab angle can be made on subsequent trials until the proper track is maintained.

ACCEPTABLE PERFORMANCE FOR EIGHTS AROUND PYLONS

The pilot must maneuver the airplane so both loops of the eight are of equal size. Performance is evaluated on proper wind drift correction, airspeed control, coordination, altitude control, and vigilance for other aircraft. Deviation of 100 feet from the selected altitude is considered disqualifying unless corrected promptly. Excessively steep banks, flight below the minimum safe altitude prescribed by regulations, or inadequate clearance from other aircraft also is disqualifying.

SECTION C - S-TURNS ACROSS A ROAD AND TURNS ABOUT A POINT

Two of the most commonly practiced ground reference maneuvers are S-turns across a road and turns about a point. It should be emphasized that the turns about a point are ground reference maneuvers. The steep turns practiced at altitude are made at a constant angle of bank with no attempt to describe a particular ground track.

S-TURNS

A road that is perpendicular to the wind should be used for performance of S-turns. The objective is to fly two perfect half circles of equal size on opposite sides of the road, as shown in figure 3-18. The illustration shows that the S-turn is two halves of a constant radius turn in which the direction is changed midway through the maneuver.

Figure 3-19 represents the airplane and the resulting ground track as they appear from above. As with most ground reference maneuvers, the pilot enters the maneuver on a downwind heading at an altitude of approximately 600 feet AGL. As the road is crossed, he rolls into a bank immediately. Since the airplane is flying downwind, it is at its highest groundspeed; therefore, the angle of bank selected at this point is the steepest used throughout the maneuver. As shown in the left portion of the illustration, the bank is then gradually reduced to trace a half circle. The roll-out should be timed so the airplane is rolled level, headed directly upwind, and is perpendicular to the road just as the road is crossed.

As the airplane crosses the road, the pilot smoothly and gradually rolls into a turn in the opposite direction. This portion of the maneuver requires the *shallowest bank* and has the *slowest groundspeed*, since the airplane is headed upwind. The bank is steepened gradually throughout the turn to continue tracing a half-circle track in the same shape and size as the one on the opposite side of

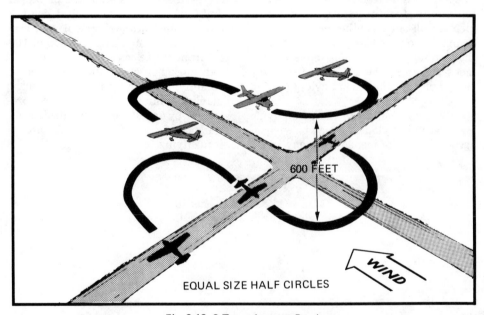

600 FEET

EQUAL SIZE HALF CIRCLES

WIND

Fig. 3-18. S-Turns Across a Road

the road. The steepest bank is attained just before rollout and the "S" is completed as the airplane crosses the road perpendicularly with the wings level.

Figure 3-20 illustrates that the airplane must be crabbed to maintain the desired ground track. During the turn from the downwind portion of the "S," the nose of the airplane is crabbed to the inside of the turn. Similarly, during the upwind turn, the airplane is crabbed to the outside of the turn to maintain proper drift correction.

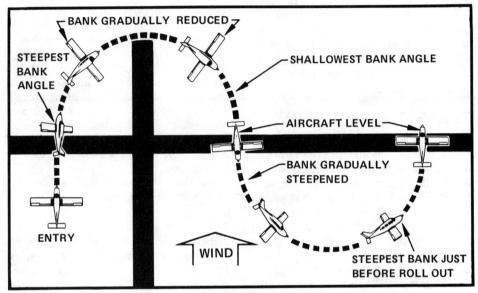

Fig. 3-19. Maintaining Track by Varying Bank Angle

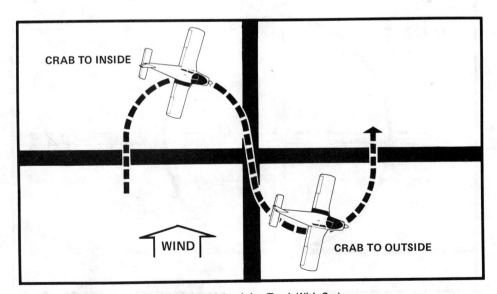

Fig. 3-20. Maintaining Track With Crab

ACCEPTABLE PERFORMANCE FOR S-TURNS

The pilot must readily select ground references and maneuver the airplane in relation to these references. Properly coordinated turns, smooth control usage, and division of attention are required. Deviation of 100 feet from the selected altitude is considered disqualifying unless corrected promptly. Excessively steep banks, flight below the minimum safe altitudes prescribed by regulations, or inadequate clearance of other aircraft is disqualifying.

TURNS ABOUT A POINT

The technique for performing turns about a point should not be confused with the steep turns performed at altitude with a constant angle of bank. Turns about a point are ground reference maneuvers that require the pilot to perform constant radius turns around a preselected point on the ground. Further objectives are to maintain a constant altitude, maintain orientation, and roll out on the initial heading after two full

turns. The maneuver and resulting ground track are depicted in figure 3-21.

This maneuver is first practiced using a medium bank at 600 feet AGL. Higher altitudes make the planning of the flight track about the point more difficult.

The point selected as a reference should be prominent and easily distinguished, yet small enough to establish a definite location. Trees, isolated haystacks, or other small landmarks can be used, but are not as effective as intersections of roads or fencelines. These items provide effective points because the wing may momentarily block the pilot's view of the reference point during right turns. If the pilot has selected a road or fenceline intersection, he can mentally project these lines to their logical intersection and maintain his orientation.

The point selected should be in the center of an area away from livestock, buildings, or concentrations of people on the ground to prevent annoyance and undue hazard. The area selected also

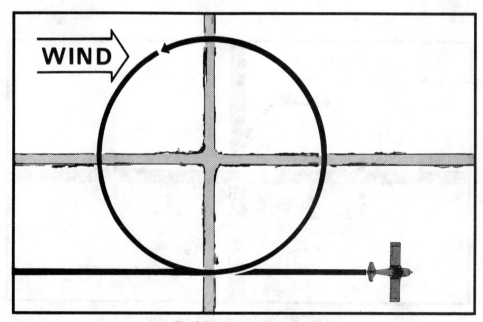

Fig. 3-21. Turns About a Point

should afford the opportunity for a safe emergency landing.

FLYING THE MANEUVER

The easiest way to enter this maneuver is to fly downwind at a distance from the point equal to the radius of the desired turn. As the pilot arrives exactly abeam the selected point, he enters a medium bank turn toward the side on which his reference point is located. He then carefully plans the track over the ground and varies the bank, as necessary, to maintain that track.

When wind exists, it is necessary to enter the steepest bank immediately, since the airplane is headed directly downwind. Then, the bank is shallowed gradually until the point where the airplane is headed directly upwind. At this position, the bank is steepened gradually until the original bank angle is reached at the point of entry. This procedure is repeated through another 360° of turn and the roll-out is made on the original entry heading.

As experience is gained, the pilot should practice turns about a point in both directions. Additionally, he should practice entering the maneuver at any point. He should understand that the angle of bank at any given point is dependent on the radius of the circle being flown, the wind velocity, and the groundspeed. When entering the maneuver at a point other than directly downwind, the angle of bank and the radius of the turn must be selected carefully in terms of wind velocity and groundspeed so an excessively steep bank angle is not required to maintain the proper ground track.

ACCEPTABLE PERFORMANCE FOR TURNS ABOUT A POINT

The pilot must maneuver the airplane so that the ground track is a constant distance from the reference point. Performance is evaluated on the basis of proper wind drift correction, airspeed control, coordination, altitude control, and vigilance for other aircraft. Deviation of more than 100 feet from the selected altitude is considered disqualifying unless corrected promptly. Excessively steep banks, flight below the minimum safe altitude prescribed by regulations, or inadequate clearance from other aircraft also is disqualifying.

chapter 4

SLIPS, TAKEOFFS, AND LANDINGS

INTRODUCTION

Few aspects of pilot training are as satisfying and rewarding as mastery of the procedures involved in takeoffs and landings. While learning slips, takeoffs, and landings, the pilot must apply all of the basic skills acquired in the early phases of the training program. Each takeoff and landing is a new challenge for the pilot. In addition to varying wind conditions, the runway surface, length, and obstructions differ at every airport the pilot visits. These factors combine to modify each takeoff and landing situation. When the pilot masters the basic traffic pattern skills, he is well prepared for takeoffs and landings under this wide variety of conditions.

SECTION A - SLIPS

The slip is a flight attitude used to increase the angle of descent without causing an increase in airspeed. This is accomplished by exposing as much of the airplane surface to the oncoming air as possible, so that the airplane's frontal area produces considerable drag. This allows a steeper angle of descent without acceleration. Flaps serve the same purpose, but they cannot always be used because of crosswinds or gusts.

As shown in figure 4-1, the pilot can execute either a *forward slip* or a *side slip*. The two types of slips are aerodynamically the same, but they differ in the way the airplane is maneuvered with respect to the ground.

FORWARD SLIP

To initiate a forward slip, one wing is lowered using aileron control and opposite rudder is applied simultaneously to keep the airplane from turning in the direction of the lowered wing. This procedure keeps the airplane's ground track in alignment with the extended centerline of the runway, but allows the nose of the airplane to angle away from the runway, as shown in figure 4-2. To prevent the airspeed from increasing, the nose is raised slightly above the normal gliding position. In this attitude, the glide path steepens even though the airspeed remains constant.

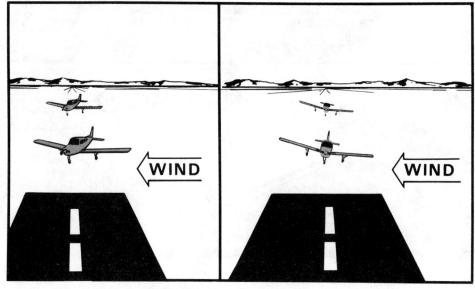

Fig. 4-1. Forward and Side Slips

Fig. 4-2. Forward Slip

As soon as sufficient altitude is lost, the recovery is accomplished by raising the low wing and simultaneously easing rudder pressure as the wings are leveled and pitch attitude is adjusted to the normal glide attitude. If the control force on the rudder is removed abruptly, the nose will swing too quickly into line and the airplane will tend to acquire excess speed.

The forward slip can be valuable when landing in fields with obstructions, since the pilot has an excellent view of the landing area during the entire slip. In an airplane with side-by-side seating, it usually is more comfortable to slip toward the pilot's side, since the structure of the airplane provides something to lean against. However, if a crosswind is present, the slip should be executed into the wind.

The only difference between the control application in right and left slips is that the control pressures are reversed. Forward slips should be performed with the engine at idle power because the use of power decreases the rate of descent.

SIDE SLIP

The side slip normally is used to compensate for drift during crosswind landings. During a side slip in a no-wind condition, the nose of the airplane remains on the same heading throughout the maneuver, but the ground track is sideways in the direction of the low wing. However, when a crosswind is present, and a side slip is performed *into* the wind, the resulting ground track is a straight line, as shown in figure 4-3. This line is parallel to the longitudinal axis of the airplane.

To maintain a constant heading and a straight flight path during a slip, the aileron and rudder control pressures must be balanced properly. Too much aileron or too little opposite rudder causes a turn in the direction of bank. In contrast, too much rudder or too little opposite aileron causes a yaw away from the bank. To steepen the descent, both aileron and rudder must be increased in a coordinated, proportionate manner.

ACCEPTABLE PERFORMANCE FOR SLIPS

The airplane should be placed in either the forward or side slip configuration smoothly, without erratic control usage. The airplane should maintain the desired track across the ground with coordinated control changes to compensate for drift. The return to normal glide attitude should be accomplished smoothly and with coordinated control usage.

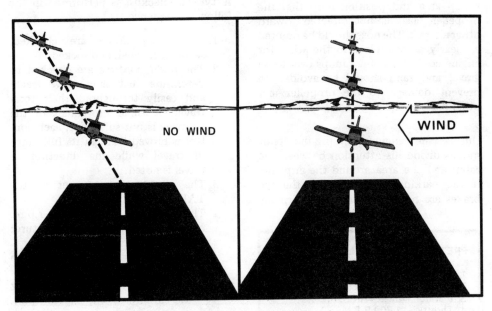

NO WIND

WIND

Fig. 4-3. Side Slip

SECTION B - NORMAL AND CROSSWIND TAKEOFFS

PRETAKEOFF CHECK

Prior to each takeoff, it is important for the pilot to perform a pretakeoff check of the airplane equipment and systems to insure proper operation. This pretakeoff check should be accomplished using a written checklist provided by the airplane manufacturer or operator. This insures that each item is checked in the proper sequence and that nothing is omitted. A typical pretakeoff checklist is shown in figure 4-4.

Before starting the pretakeoff checklist, the pilot should taxi the airplane to the runup area and position it so that the propeller blast is not directed toward other aircraft. The nose should be pointed as nearly as possible into the wind for engine cooling. Engine runups over loose gravel and sand should be avoided to prevent damage to the propeller and other parts of the airplane.

During the engine runup, the pilot should divide his attention between the cabin and the area around the airplane. If the parking brake slips or the toe brakes are not held firmly, the airplane

can move forward while the pilot's attention is diverted inside the cabin.

The engine normally will have warmed sufficiently before the pretakeoff check so that it will accelerate smoothly when power is applied to check the carburetor heat, ignition, and mixture. All engine instrument indications must be normal before takeoff. If any abnormal condition is observed during the runup, the airplane should be returned for maintenance, since even minor malfunctions can affect the safety and efficiency of the flight.

A typical checklist is performed in the following sequence.

1. The *cabin doors* are checked, securely latched, and locked.
2. The *flight controls* are checked to determine that they move freely and easily throughout their total travel. A small movement of the controls is not sufficient; each control is moved through its full range of travel while the direction of travel is noted.
3. The *elevator trim* is set to the TAKEOFF position.
4. The *throttle* is set to the r.p.m. recommended by the manufacturer for the power check.
   a. The carburetor heat is pulled to the ON position and the power loss noted. With hot air entering the carburetor, the engine r.p.m. decreases, indicating the carburetor heat is functioning.
   b. The magnetos are tested by noting the r.p.m. with the magneto switch in the BOTH position, then moving the magneto switch to the RIGHT position and noting the r.p.m. Next, the magneto switch is returned to BOTH, then switched to the LEFT position and the r.p.m.

PRETAKEOFF CHECKLIST

1. Cabin Doors — LATCHED
2. Flight Controls — FREE and CORRECT
3. Elevator Trim — TAKEOFF
4. Throttle — 1,700 R.P.M.
   a. Carburetor Heat — CHECK (for r.p.m. drop)
   b. Magnetos — CHECK (r.p.m. drop of no more than 150 r.p.m. on either magneto or 75 r.p.m. differential between magnetos)
   c. Engine Instruments and Ammeter — CHECK
   d. Suction Gauge — CHECK
5. Flight Instruments and Radios — SET

Fig. 4-4. Typical Pretakeoff Checklist

noted. The magneto switch should be returned to the BOTH position for takeoff. Permissible r.p.m. reductions are specified by the airplane manufacturer. However, one magneto should not show a drop of more than 75 r.p.m. compared with the drop of the other magneto.

c. Engine instruments are checked and should indicate operation in the green arcs.

d. The suction gauge is checked for a normal indication (usually 4.6 to 5.4 inches of mercury). A low reading usually indicates a dirty air filter. Unreliable gyro indications may result if sufficient suction is not maintained.

5. The *flight instruments* and *radios* are checked and set.

a. The altimeter is set to the airport barometric reading, as supplied by the tower controller, or to indicate the correct field elevation if operating from an uncontrolled field.

b. The heading indicator is set to coincide with the magnetic compass indication.

c. All gyro instruments are checked for stable operation.

d. The radios are turned on and set to the desired frequencies.

e. The course selectors are set to the desired courses or radials.

When the checklist is complete, the pilot is ready for takeoff. When operating from an uncontrolled field, a 360° taxiing turn should be performed in the direction of the traffic pattern to observe the entire area for other traffic. When the area is clear, the airplane can be taxied to the takeoff position. At controlled airports, takeoff clearance is obtained from the control tower.

TAXIING INTO TAKEOFF POSITION

When ready for takeoff, the pilot should taxi to the end of the runway, line up with the runway centerline, center the nosewheel, and neutralize the ailerons.

After checking the windsock once again to determine the wind position in relation to the runway, the pilot is ready to begin the takeoff.

The right hand is placed on the throttle and should remain there throughout the takeoff. This assures that the throttle does not vibrate back during the takeoff roll and allows the pilot to close the throttle quickly if a decision is made to abort the takeoff roll.

The feet should be resting on the floor with the balls of the feet on the bottom edges of the rudder pedals. This places the feet in a position where they have no tendency to inadvertently press the toe brakes.

TAKEOFF PROCEDURES

The takeoff roll begins with a *smooth* application of power. As soon as power is applied and the airplane begins to roll, the pilot should select an object beyond the end of the runway, in line with the runway centerline, to use as a reference for directional control. Additionally, the power instruments are checked to insure that the engine is developing full power.

During the takeoff roll, directional control is maintained with the rudder pedals and aileron control is used for wing position. If the wind is straight down the runway, the pilot should hold neutral aileron. The rudder pedals are sufficient to maintain directional control even at slow speed; however, the rudder itself becomes more effective as speed increases. Because of this factor, the amount of rudder deflection required for directional control changes throughout the takeoff roll. Prior to adding power, the rudder is neutral. When power is added, right rudder pressure is applied to counteract engine torque. As speed increases and the controls become more effective, rudder pressure is reduced to maintain directional control and slight back pressure is applied to the control wheel. As the airplane approaches liftoff speed, elevator responsiveness becomes sufficient to make the nosewheel light on the ground. The takeoff attitude is established at this time. In most training airplanes, this attitude is similar to the normal climb attitude.

The takeoff attitude is important because it is a compromise between holding the nose on the ground and selecting an attitude which is too nose-high. With the nosewheel on the ground, the airplane tends to build excess airspeed, which increases the length of runway required for takeoff. With an excessively nose-high attitude, the airplane may be forced into the air prematurely, then settle back to the runway, or it may be

at such a high angle of attack (high drag condition) that it cannot accelerate to the liftoff airspeed. With the proper attitude, the airplane attains a safe speed and becomes airborne near the proper climb speed. If that attitude is held after liftoff, the airplane rapidly accelerates to climb speed. Another advantage of maintaining this attitude is that if the airplane is lifted into the air prematurely by a wind gust, it will be in the best attitude to accelerate to climb speed. In addition, if the airplane settles, it can safely touch the runway and continue the takeoff roll.

When the airplane reaches climb speed, the nose attitude is adjusted to the proper climb attitude. After liftoff, the takeoff leg of the traffic pattern is flown straight out on an extension of the centerline of the runway without drifting to one side or the other. When remaining in the traffic pattern, the turn to crosswind can be initiated at an altitude of approximately 700 feet AGL (depending on atmospheric conditions, traffic, and the airport layout), unless other traffic requires additional spacing. To depart the pattern, the pilot may continue straight out or perform a 45° turn after reaching traffic pattern altitude.

CROSSWIND TAKEOFF

During practice of takeoffs, one of the factors which must be considered is the effect of a crosswind. Each airplane has a maximum safe crosswind component at which it may be operated. The term *crosswind component* refers to that part of the wind velocity that acts at right angles to the airplane's path on takeoff or landing.

A typical crosswind component chart is shown in figure 4-5. This chart is applicable to a specific airplane and indicates that it may be operated at a maximum direct crosswind of 17-1/2 knots. It is possible to take off with the wind velocity higher than 17-1/2 knots, pro-

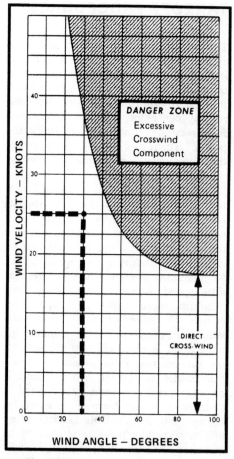

Fig. 4-5. Maximum Safe Crosswind Chart

viding the crosswind component does not exceed this amount. For example, a 25-knot wind at an angle of 30° to the runway does not exceed the maximum allowable crosswind component. This is illustrated by the intersection of the vertical and horizontal dashed lines in figure 4-5. The chart shows that as the angle of the wind to the runway decreases, the danger from an excessive crosswind component decreases.

During the takeoff and landing rolls, a crosswind tends to push and roll the airplane to the downwind side of the runway, as shown in figure 4-6, position 1. To compensate for this effect, the ailerons are used in the same manner as for crosswind taxiing.

Due to the ineffectiveness of the flight controls at slow airspeeds, *full aileron deflection* should be used at the beginning of the takeoff roll. The wind flow over the wing with the raised aileron tends to hold that wing down, while airflow under the wing with the lowered aileron tends to push that wing up. These factors counteract the rolling tendency caused by the crosswind, as shown in figure 4-6, position 2.

As the airplane accelerates, the ailerons become more effective. Therefore the

deflection should be reduced gradually so that it is just sufficient to counteract the rolling tendency. As shown in figure 4-6, position 1, wind also attempts to weathervane the airplane. This effect is counteracted by rudder application.

The weathervaning tendency is a result of the wind striking the rudder surface, which is a considerable distance from the center of gravity. This causes the nose of the airplane to turn into the wind.

The amount of crosswind correction necessary depends on the crosswind component. With moderate crosswind components, the airplane is sensitive to side loads as it approaches liftoff speed. If the corrections are improper, side loads can be placed on the landing gear.

Determining how much aileron and rudder is required to compensate for a crosswind requires practice. When the right amount is obtained, the pilot feels no side load and the airplane tracks straight down the runway.

The technique for a crosswind takeoff is illustrated in figure 4-7. First, the pilot aligns the airplane with the centerline of the runway and applies full aileron into

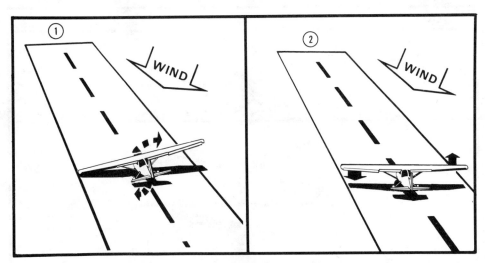

Fig. 4-6. Effects of Crosswind During Takeoff

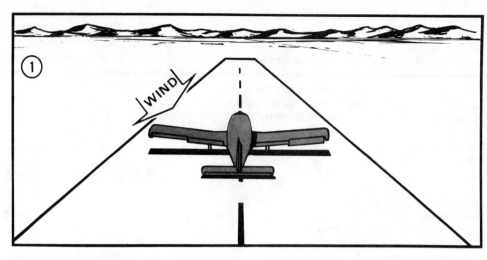

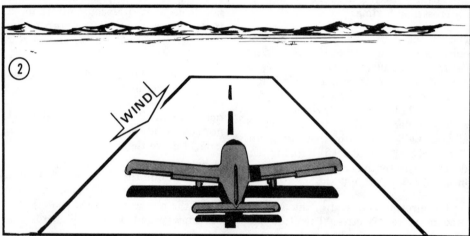

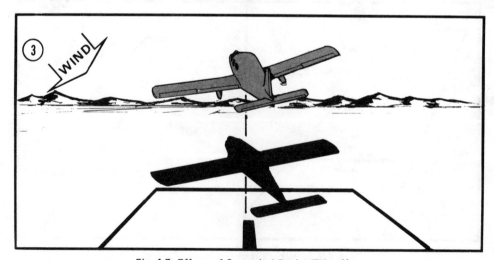

Fig. 4-7. Effects of Crosswind During Takeoff

the wind, as shown at position 1. Full power is applied in the normal manner. Then, as speed increases and ailerons become effective, aileron pressure is reduced until there is just enough to counteract the crosswind (position 2). The airplane is held on the runway until a slightly higher-than-normal liftoff speed is attained. At this point, the airplane is lifted off the runway promptly and established in a normal climb attitude. This technique reduces the chance of the airplane being lifted off the runway prematurely by a sudden gust of wind before it has attained sufficient airspeed to remain airborne.

When the airplane is airborne and a positive rate of climb is established, a crab is entered by making a coordinated turn *into* the wind. This technique allows the airplane to track straight out on an imaginary extension of the runway centerline, as shown in figure 4-7, position 3.

ACCEPTABLE PERFORMANCE FOR TAKEOFFS

The performance of normal and crosswind takeoffs is evaluated on the basis of power application, smoothness, wind drift correction, coordination, and directional control. The pilot should maintain climb speed within five knots of the desired climb speed.

SIMULATED TAKEOFF EMERGENCIES

Although an engine malfunction on takeoff is rare, the possibility does exist. Therefore, ways to handle this situation are presented during flight training. The simulated emergency situation occurs when the instructor reduces engine power by closing the throttle suddenly.

The objective of this practice is to prepare the pilot to meet the problems of a forced landing on takeoff. It helps develop judgment, technique, confidence, and the ability to respond quickly and accurately to situations requiring prompt action.

The first factor that must be considered is the possibility of an engine malfunction on the takeoff roll or just after liftoff. If the pilot suspects a malfunction during the takeoff roll, he should abort the takeoff quickly by moving the throttle to the idle position. The brakes are used, as necessary, to slow the airplane and the rudder is used to maintain directional control.

If the airplane has become airborne when the simulated emergency occurs and sufficient runway is available for landing, the pilot should reduce the attitude slightly and allow the airplane to settle back on the runway. Generally, if the airplane is below 400 feet AGL and power is lost, the pilot has no choice but to continue straight ahead, making only small changes in direction to avoid obstacles. This technique is necessary because insufficient altitude is available to make a power-off 180° turn to return to the airport for a landing.

During training, the pilot is exposed to and trained in many possible emergency situations. Many or all of the simulated emergencies practiced will never occur, but the practice received is valuable in learning the characteristics of the airplane and building confidence so when the pilot is alone, he is able to handle the airplane in a wide variety of situations.

SECTION C - NORMAL AND CROSSWIND LANDINGS

The approach and landing is the phase of flight most pilots look forward to because it represents a high degree of accomplishment. Success in landings does not eliminate the need for further flight instruction. However, proper execution of landings is important because it provides an indication of the pilot's ability to execute basic maneuvers, plan, think ahead of the airplane, and divide his attention among several tasks.

APPROACH AND LANDING

A landing is nothing more than the transition of the airplane from an airborne vehicle to a ground vehicle. A successful landing requires the use of procedures and techniques that consistently result in landing the airplane on the desired area without violating good safety practices. This requires a high degree of planning that begins on the downwind leg. For example, the pilot of the airplane shown in figure 4-8 plans to touch down on a preselected area or point on the runway. Several factors will influence the airplane's movement during the approach to that point.

The distance traveled from point 1 to point 2 varies with the airplane's distance from the runway on the downwind

and base legs. Wind and airspeed influence how fast the airplane flies that distance, while power, airspeed, and flap position influence the rate of descent.

If the pilot uses a different traffic pattern size, airspeed, flap setting, or rate of turn to base and final on each approach, he has a new problem to solve on each approach. His chances of touching down consistently at the appropriate spot on the runway are reduced considerably. To preclude this situation, one goal in the traffic pattern and in approach-to-landing practice is to eliminate as many of the variables as possible.

An attempt should be made to fly a consistent traffic pattern so the distance of the downwind leg from the runway does not vary. In addition, altitude, point of power reduction, and approach airspeed should be the same for each approach.

The turns to base and final at the points indicated in figure 4-9 should be consistent. Then, flaps and power can be used to make minor corrections for position and wind influences.

Throughout training, the pilot should practice consistency and exercise precise control of the airplane to reduce the number of variables in the landing ap-

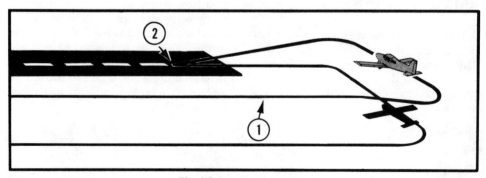

Fig. 4-8. Landing Approach

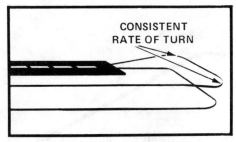

CONSISTENT
RATE OF TURN

*Fig. 4-9. Turns to Base and Final
Should Be Consistent*

proach. A typical approach and landing is described in the following paragraphs.

DOWNWIND LEG

As illustrated in figure 4-10, the downwind leg is flown at a distance of approximately one-half mile from the runway in use. The airplane's track should parallel the runway with no tendency to angle toward or drift away from the runway. Angling or drifting causes the traffic pattern to have an abnormal shape which greatly influences the length of the base leg.

180° POINT

When approaching the point opposite the area of intended landing, or the 180° point, the airspeed should be near cruise in light trainers (or at a reduced cruise speed for higher performance airplanes). In addition, altitude should be at the designated traffic pattern altitude.

Just before reaching the 180° point, the pilot performs the prelanding checklist. At the 180° point, the power is reduced to the descent power setting, altitude is maintained, and airspeed is allowed to slow to approach speed. (See Fig. 4-11.)

BEGINNING THE DESCENT

When the airplane reaches approach airspeed, that speed should be maintained and the descent initiated. The transition from cruise speed on downwind to descent speed is a practical application of the transition from cruise to descent introduced in the practice area. The recommended descent or approach speed generally is specified by the airplane manufacturer.

If an approach speed range from 70 to 80 knots is recommended, the pilot should select a speed in this range and maintain a pitch attitude that produces that speed as precisely as possible. If an approach speed is not recommended, a final approach speed that is 1.3 times the power-off stall speed in landing configuration can be used.

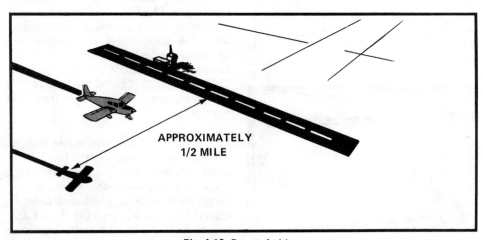

APPROXIMATELY
1/2 MILE

Fig. 4-10. Downwind Leg

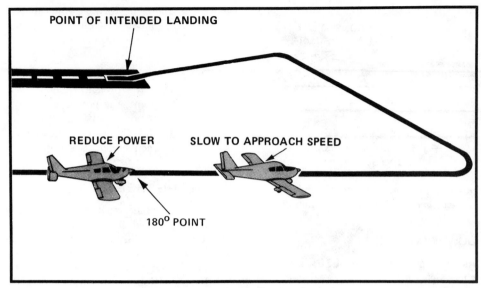

POINT OF INTENDED LANDING

REDUCE POWER   SLOW TO APPROACH SPEED

180° POINT

Fig. 4-11. 180° Point

BASE LEG

The turn to base leg usually begins after the airplane has descended approximately 200 to 400 feet; however, the best cue for determining when to begin the turn is obtained from the airplane's position relative to the runway. The runway should appear to be between 30° and 45° behind the wing and look similar to the view shown in figure 4-12.

With practice, this perspective becomes so familiar that the pilot can detect the need for small corrections at this position. The start of the turn to base leg should be varied to compensate for variations in conditions. For example, if the downwind leg is wider than normal,

Fig. 4-12. Begin Turn to Base Leg

the turn should be started a little sooner, as shown in figure 4-13. As experience is gained, it becomes easier to judge these variations.

Throughout the approach, the pilot must be alert for other traffic in the pattern. He should always check for other airplanes on final approach.

KEY POSITION

When the airplane rolls out on base leg, it is at the point called the key position. (See Fig. 4-14.) When the key position is reached on each approach to a landing, the pilot must assess his position and determine whether or not corrections must be made in the approach pattern. This assessment is based on four factors —altitude, airspeed, distance from the runway, and wind.

For example, if the airplane is high, it will land beyond the desired touchdown point. In this situation, there are three possible corrections—the pilot can reduce power, extend additional flaps, or extend the base leg. (See Fig. 4-15.) Any one or all three can be used, depending upon the amount of correction needed.

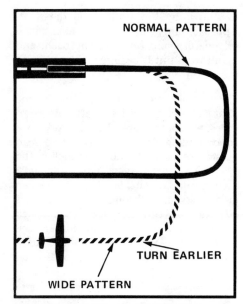

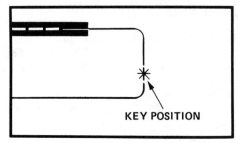

Fig. 4-14. Key Position

Fig. 4-13. Wider-Than-Normal Pattern

If the airplane is low or wide on base leg, or the wind is stronger than normal, the airplane will land short of the desired point if no corrections are made. There are two actions that can be taken to avoid this situation. The pilot can begin the turn to final sooner than normal or he can add power. Either one or both can be used, depending on the amount of correction necessary. Retracting the flaps usually is not considered an accept-able correction. Normally, once flaps are extended, they are not retracted until the landing has been completed or the landing approach abandoned.

Corrections for position should be made anytime the pilot recognizes a need for a correction. The significance of the key position is that it is an early decision point where the pilot can easily make major adjustments to insure a smooth approach and avoid large or abrupt last-minute corrections. Throughout the approach, the pilot should continue to assess his position relative to the runway to determine the need for corrections. Through the process of assessing his position, making corrections, and then reevaluating the touchdown point, the pilot is able to judge his touchdown point accurately.

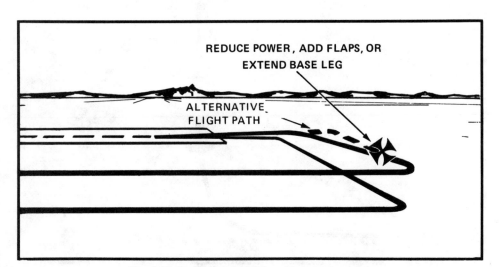

Fig. 4-15. Correction for High or Close-In Approach

FINAL APPROACH

Before turning to the final approach leg, the pilot always should look in all directions for other traffic, since an aircraft on final has the right-of-way over other aircraft in the traffic pattern. If the area is clear, the turn to final can be made. This turn should be a coordinated maneuver, performed at approximately 400 feet AGL.

The turn to final also should be planned so the airplane rolls out on an extension of the runway centerline. The final approach should neither angle to the runway, as shown by the airplane on the left in figure 4-16, nor require an S-turn, as shown by the airplane on the right. Approach airspeed should be maintained in the turn and on final approach, and monitored until beginning the landing transition.

Throughout the landing approach, the pilot's ability to use visual attitude references to control speed is the key to a good landing. He must be able to scan outside references while controlling the speed accurately. The pilot is encouraged to look outside since, if he can judge airspeed through the airplane's attitude, he can exercise better speed control and perform smoother approaches. The nose attitudes should look familiar, since they are the ones used

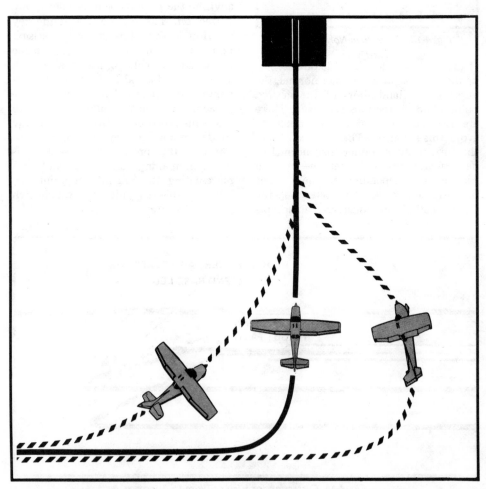

Fig. 4-16. Turn to Final Should Produce Roll-Out on Runway Centerline

when practicing straight descents and descending turns.

If the pilot maintains a constant approach angle, the apparent shape of the runway will remain fixed. If the approach becomes shallower, the runway will appear to shorten and become wider. Conversely, if the approach is steepened, the runway will appear to be longer and narrower. (See Fig. 4-17.) Therefore, if the pilot maintains a constant approach angle, the sides of the runway will maintain the same relationship and the threshold will remain in a fixed position in relation to the airplane's nose.

During early landing practice, it is common for the pilot to overcontrol and make corrections that are in excess of the required amounts. As a guide, the pilot should visualize the normal or standard pattern and make smooth, positive corrections back to that pattern. If he is low, for example, it usually is not necessary to make an abrupt correction and climb back to the standard pattern. Instead, he can reduce the rate of descent or use level flight for a short period until the desired approach angle is regained.

If the airplane is low and slow, power must be added and the nose lowered. Lowering the nose when the airplane is low is sometimes a difficult response that must be practiced and learned.

Approach speed is frequently near the best angle-of-glide speed. This means that any other airspeed results in a higher rate of descent. If the airplane is short of the desired touchdown spot, the pilot cannot stretch a glide by raising the nose and slowing the airspeed; instead, power must be added.

If the approach is extremely high, there is very little value in entering a steep descent. Although it appears the airplane will reach the desired point of touchdown, the dive causes an excessive airspeed which must be dissipated in the flareout. The result is that a greater distance is covered as the airplane floats down the runway, usually well beyond the desired landing point.

LANDING

The landing consists of the flareout to reduce speed and decrease the rate of descent, the touchdown, and the rollout. The term *flareout* means the process

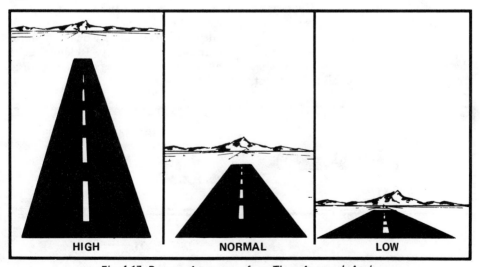

HIGH NORMAL LOW

Fig. 4-17. Runway Appearance from Three Approach Angles

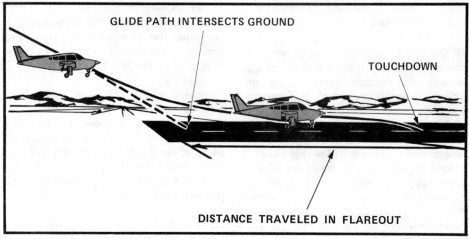

Fig. 4-18. Flareout Distance

of changing the attitude of the airplane from a glide or descent attitude to a landing attitude. Other terms used interchangeably for this maneuver are flare, roundout, and leveloff.

The point at which the airplane actually touches down can be estimated by finding the point where the glide path intersects the ground and adding the approximate distance to be traveled in the flareout. The glide path intersection is the point on the ground that has no apparent relative movement. As the airplane descends, all objects beyond the glide path intersection point appear to move away from the airplane, while objects closer appear to move toward the airplane. The approximate distance traveled in the flareout varies somewhat from the glide path intersection point,

depending on the approach speed and wind. For example, if the pilot wishes to touch down at the point shown in figure 4-18, his apparent aiming point for the glide path should be approximately 150 feet short of that point.

The flareout begins at different altitudes for airplanes of varying weights and approach speeds. However, for most training airplanes, it begins at approximately 15 feet AGL. The flareout is initiated with a gradual increase in back pressure on the control wheel to reduce speed and decrease the rate of descent. Ideally, the airplane reaches a zero rate of descent approximately one foot above the runway at about 8 to 10 knots above stall speed, with idle power. (See Fig. 4-19.)

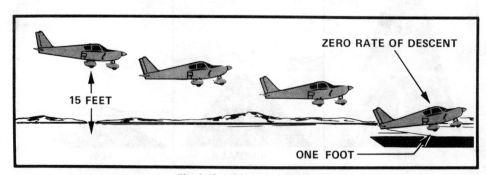

Fig. 4-19. Initiation of Flareout

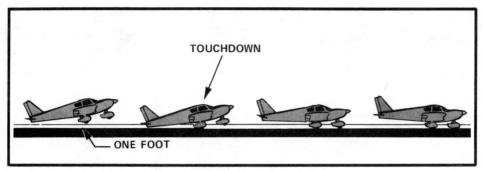

Fig. 4-20. Attitude at Flareout

Then, the pilot simply attempts to hold the airplane just off the runway by increasing the elevator back pressure. This causes the airplane to settle slowly to the runway in a slightly nose-high attitude as it approaches stall speed. The pitch attitude at touchdown should be very close to the pitch attitude at take-off, with no weight on the nose gear. As shown in figure 4-20, back pressure on the control wheel should be maintained until the nosewheel touches down, then slowly relaxed.

The cues the pilot uses in the flareout and landing are a combination of visual and kinesthetic feelings. Descents and approaches to stalls have been practiced to build sensitivity to control responses and smoothness in preparation for the flare and landing. Generally, kinesthetic sensitivity is not developed fully at the time landing practice begins; therefore, vision is the most important sense.

The altitude for the flareout and the height throughout the flareout are determined by the pilot's depth perception. Depth perception is the visual comparison of the size of known objects on the ground; therefore, where the pilot focuses his vision during the approach is important. If he focuses too close to the airplane or looks straight down, the airspeed blurs objects on the ground, causing his actions to be delayed or too abrupt. The tendency when focusing too close is to overcontrol and level off too high.

If the pilot focuses too far down the runway, he is unable to judge height above the ground accurately and, consequently, his reactions are slow. In this situation, the pilot generally allows the airplane to fly onto the runway without flaring. Thus, it becomes obvious that the pilot must focus at some intermediate point. A guideline is to focus about the same distance ahead of the airplane as when driving a car at the same speed. (See Fig. 4-21.)

During the landing, the airplane should be pointed straight down the runway. When flying an airplane with side-by-side seating, the reference point for sighting over the nose is not the center of the nose, but a point directly in front of the pilot's eyes. If the pilot sights over the center of the nose, he tends to land the airplane in a crab, which places heavy side loads on the landing gear.

Directional control is maintained during the roll-out with rudder pressure. As the airplane touches down, the feet should be in the same position on the rudder pedals as they were during the takeoff. With the heels on the floor, there is no tendency to inadvertently use the brakes, but the pilot is able to reach them, if necessary.

GO-AROUND

A general rule of thumb used in landing practice is that if the airplane has not

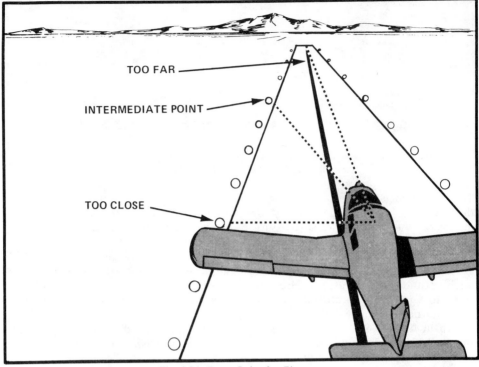

Fig. 4-21. Focus Point for Flareout

touched down in the first one-third of the runway, the pilot should abandon the landing by flying around the traffic pattern and setting up another landing approach. A go-around also may be required when an aircraft or some other obstacle is on the runway or when the pilot feels the approach is uncomfortable, incorrect, or potentially dangerous.

The decision to make a go-around should be positive and the maneuver should be initiated before a critical situation develops. When the decision is made, it should be carried out without hesitation. In many cases, the go-around is initiated with the airplane at a slow airspeed and in a nose-high attitude. The first response should be to apply all available power and adjust the pitch attitude to a normal climb attitude. However, the airplane should be accelerated to the best angle-of-climb speed before the climb is started and the flaps should be retracted slowly. Flaps always should be

retracted with care, since, at low speeds, it is possible for the airplane to stall or lose altitude if the flaps are retracted too rapidly.

If another aircraft is on the runway during the go-around, a gentle turn should be made to the right side of the runway, as shown in figure 4-22. Special cases, such as use of parallel runways, may prevent this slight turn or may require a slight left turn. The flight path should be far enough to the side of the runway that it does not interfere with an airplane taking off. In this position, the pilot can see the runway clearly and avoid flying directly over any traffic taking off.

The climb on the takeoff leg should be continued parallel to the runway until the crosswind leg is reached. If another airplane is ahead, the pilot should allow proper spacing and join the traffic pattern.

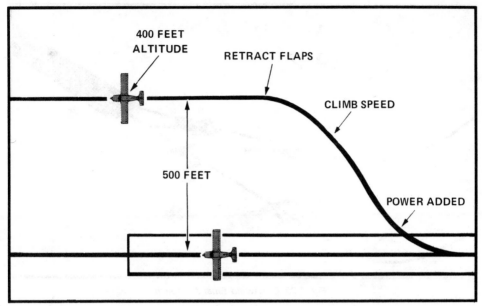

Fig. 4-22. Go-Around

BOUNCED LANDING

At times, the pilot may perform poor landings that cause the airplane to bounce into the air. Usually, it is wise not to attempt to salvage these landings. Instead, the pilot should make an immediate go-around. Except when lowering flaps or trimming the airplane, the pilot should have his hand on the throttle throughout the approach and landing. When a landing is bad, a decision should be made to go around and all available power added. The pitch attitude is adjusted to a normal climb attitude and the go-around procedures are completed.

If the airplane bounces only a small amount and just a few feet of altitude are gained, the nose should be placed in the landing attitude while the airplane settles back to the runway. The same procedure should be used if the airplane "balloons" because the elevator has been pulled back too rapidly. The nose should be returned to the landing attitude and held in that attitude until the airplane settles on the runway. However, if there is any question about the successful outcome of the landing, the best procedure is to go around.

USE OF WING FLAPS DURING LANDING

Landings can be made with partial flaps, full flaps, or no flaps. The procedures used with various flap settings are generally the same; however, there are specific differences. With no flaps, the rate of descent usually is less than with partial flaps, so the approach tends to be high and long. To avoid this situation, power and the traffic pattern must be adjusted. Since the stall speed with no flaps is higher than with full flaps, the airplane touches down at a faster speed and the landing roll-out is longer.

When full flaps are used for landing, one-third flaps normally are extended on the downwind leg and two-thirds flaps are extended on base leg. Normally, the extension to the full-flap position is performed on the final approach leg.

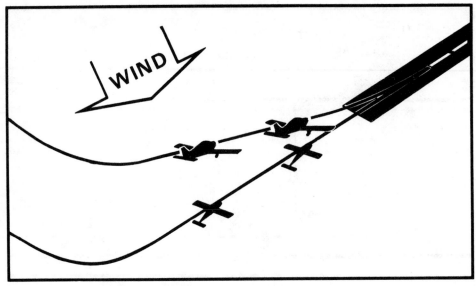

Fig. 4-23. Crosswind Final Approach

At the full-flap setting, the rate of descent increases so the tendency is to land short. The touchdown speed is slower, since the full-flap stall speed is less than the partial-flap or no-flap stall speed. This results in a shorter ground roll.

If a go-around with full flaps is required, the pilot should follow the procedures previously described. After adding all available power, the pilot should not attempt to enter a normal climb attitude immediately. Instead, he should use the straight-and-level, full-flap, slow flight attitude which allows the airplane to maintain its present altitude. As the best angle-of-climb speed is approached, the flaps can be raised slowly. As the airplane accelerates and the airspeed gradually increases, the pitch attitude should

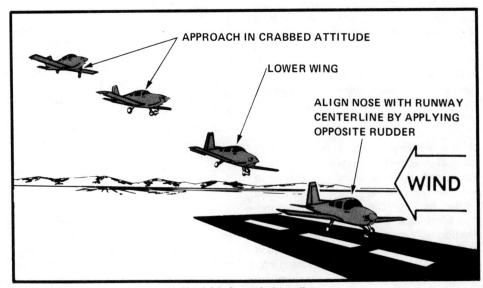

Fig. 4-24. Crosswind Landing

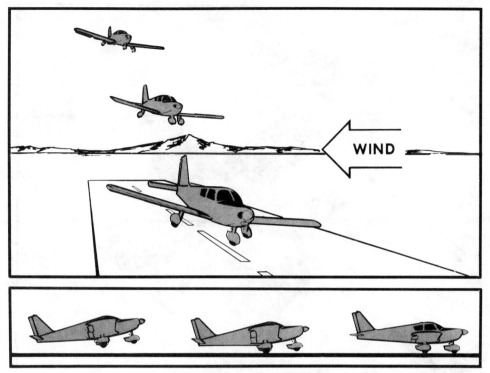

Fig. 4-25. Crosswind Landing Flareout

be adjusted to the climb attitude. An attempt to raise the nose immediately in a full-flap go-around may result in a stall. In addition, suddenly raising the flaps can cause the airplane to descend onto the ground.

CROSSWIND LANDING TECHNIQUE

The approach to landing in a crosswind is essentially the crosswind takeoff process in reverse. As illustrated in figure 4-23, the turn to final should be completed on an extension of the runway centerline with the airplane in a crab to correct for wind drift.

On final, the wing is lowered into the wind and opposite rudder pressure is used to keep the nose pointed straight down the runway. When the slip is performed properly, the airplane has no tendency to drift from one side of the runway to the other.

Beginning pilots usually place the airplane in the wing-low condition at altitudes of 100 to 200 feet while on final, but as they become more experienced, they tend to wait until just before beginning the flareout. (See Fig. 4-24.) The flare is started at the normal altitude for flareout. The wing is held down throughout the flare and touchdown, causing the airplane to touch down on one wheel, as shown in figure 4-25. The airplane must contact the runway without drifting to either side. Both the ground track and the longitudinal axis of the airplane must be aligned with the runway when the airplane contacts the ground; otherwise, extreme side loads will be imposed on the landing gear and tires, resulting in damage.

As the airplane slows, the downwind wing will lower and the other wheel will touch the ground. As the airplane continues to slow, more aileron is added, since the ailerons become less effective with speed loss.

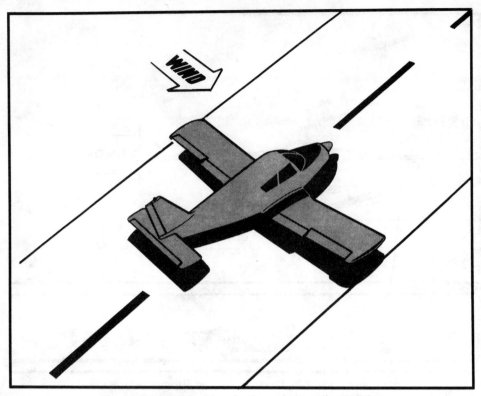

Fig. 4-26. Control Positions for Crosswind Landing Roll-Out

In moderate and light crosswinds, the nose attitude for liftoff and touchdown is the same as in normal takeoffs and landings. In a strong crosswind, the nose is placed on the ground with positive elevator pressure to allow the nosewheel to assist in directional control. Care must be taken not to lift the main landing gear off the runway as a result of excessive airspeed and forward control pressure. When the speed has slowed and the nosewheel touches the ground, positive forward elevator pressure assists in maintaining directional control. In addition, aileron controls should be fully into the wind, not neutralized, at the end of the landing roll, as shown in figure 4-26.

In gusty wind conditions, a slightly different landing technique may be used. Better control can be maintained if the airplane is flown onto the runway at an airspeed slightly higher than normal, then held on the runway with *slight* forward elevator pressure.

In a left-hand traffic pattern, when the wind is from the right side of the runway, the wind tends to distort the pattern by pushing the airplane wide on the downwind leg and slowing the groundspeed on the base leg. This condition, if not corrected, results in approaches that are short of the runway or shallow, angling turns to final.

When the wind is from the left of the landing runway heading, it tends to push the airplane closer to the runway and increase groundspeed on base leg. This situation tends to cause overshooting on final and approaches that are high and long. If the pilot recognizes these tendencies, he can make compensations in the traffic pattern.

ACCEPTABLE PERFORMANCE FOR LANDINGS

The performance of normal and crosswind landings is evaluated on the basis of landing technique, judgment, wind drift correction, coordination, power technique, and smoothness. Final approach speed should be maintained within five knots of the recommended approach speed and touchdown should be accomplished in the proper landing attitude within a specified portion of the runway or landing area. Touching down with an excessive side load on the landing gear or poor directional control is disqualifying.

chapter 5

ADVANCED MANEUVERS

INTRODUCTION

During flight training, maneuvers are introduced that cover the full scope of the airplane's handling characteristics and responses to control movements. Such maneuvers include flight at minimum controllable airspeed, approach-to-landing stalls, and steep turns. The general purpose of these maneuvers is to teach the pilot how the airplane responds and reacts in a variety of power, attitude, flap, and landing gear configurations. Practice of these maneuvers not only develops the pilot's perception, orientation, and proficiency, but also his feel for the airplane.

SECTION A - MANEUVERING AT MINIMUM CONTROLLABLE AIRSPEED

Maneuvering at minimum controllable airspeed helps the pilot develop a feel for the controls and dramatically relates load factor, attitude, airspeed, and altitude control. Knowledge of these relationships will aid the pilot in maintaining proper airspeeds and attitudes for changing flight conditions. It also helps the pilot to assess the reduction of control effectiveness during flight at slower-than-normal speeds and to determine the power required for flight at different airspeeds. Practice of flight at minimum controllable airspeed prepares the pilot for the techniques and positive control necessary during takeoff and landing practice.

MINIMUM CONTROLLABLE AIRSPEED PROCEDURES

Flight at minimum controllable airspeed is practiced at an airspeed above the stall speed. However, this speed must be sufficiently slow so any reduction in speed or an increase in load factor results in immediate indications of a stall.

The procedures for entering flight at minimum controllable airspeed from cruise flight help develop smoothness and coordination of elevator, rudder, and power controls. The initial problem is to perform a smooth transition from cruise flight attitude to the minimum

Fig. 5-1. Transition From Cruise to Minimum Controllable Airspeed

controllable airspeed attitude while maintaining altitude, as shown in figure 5-1.

The following procedure is used to enter the maneuver. Carburetor heat is applied if normally used when power is reduced, then power is reduced several hundred r.p.m. (or several inches of manifold pressure) below the power setting required to maintain altitude. After the power reduction, back pressure is applied to the control wheel to maintain altitude as the airspeed decreases. Back pressure should be applied just fast enough to maintain altitude. If the elevator pressure is applied too fast, the airplane climbs; if the application is too slow, altitude is lost. During this transition, the elevator trim tab should be used to remove the excess control back pressure.

When the airplane nears the desired attitude and airspeed, power must be increased to a setting which will maintain altitude. Small power adjustments then are made to maintain a constant altitude and the airplane is retrimmed, as necessary, to remove control pressures.

Figure 5-2 illustrates the approximate pitch attitude required during flight at minimum controllable airspeed.

As the airplane slows, the pilot also will notice that the rudder pressure requirements change. Right rudder pressure becomes necessary for proper coordination and heading control because of the left-turning tendencies caused by the high angle of attack, high torque, and pronounced P-factor. If right rudder is not applied, the airplane will turn to the left due to these tendencies. The pilot should refer to the ball of the turn coordinator to assist in determining the amount of rudder required. A feeling of pressure pushing against the body to the right also indicates that right rudder is needed. (See Fig. 5-3.)

Fig. 5-2. Pitch Attitude for Minimum Controllable Airspeed

Fig. 5-3. Rudder Requirement for Minimum Controllable Airspeed

While maneuvering at minimum controllable airspeed, there is a sensation of insufficient control response. The controls feel "mushy" and it is necessary to use greater control movements than normally required for the same attitude displacement. The response of the airplane to the control movements also is slow.

ALTITUDE AND AIRSPEED CONTROL

When performing flight at minimum controllable airspeed, the primary function of the flight controls is very apparent. An attempt to climb by applying elevator back pressure will not be successful; rather, the airspeed will decrease, immediate indications of an approaching stall will occur, and the altitude will decrease. Attempts to lose altitude by lowering the nose with the elevator will cause a decrease in altitude, but the airspeed also will increase beyond acceptable limits.

The correct procedure for regaining lost altitude is to apply power. A very small increase in pitch attitude may be necessary to maintain the desired airspeed. To lose altitude, power must be reduced in conjunction with a small reduction in pitch attitude. This relationship of power as a primary altitude control and the use of elevator as a primary airspeed control can be further clarified by an in-flight demonstration.

The student uses the throttle and the instructor takes charge of the elevator control. Then, the student is told he can use any power setting and change it as often as he desires. The instructor maintains a given airspeed, such as 60 knots, regardless of where the power is set.

If the student applies full power, the instructor simply increases elevator back pressure to adjust the pitch attitude to maintain the desired airspeed. This condition results in full power, 60-knot climb.

If the student reduces power to idle, forward elevator pressure is applied to lower the pitch attitude to maintain the desired airspeed. This results in a 60-knot power-off glide. This exercise should graphically demonstrate that when the airspeed must be maintained at a constant value, it is controlled primarily with pitch attitude.

This demonstration also should point out that with a constant airspeed, power controls altitude. With the instructor maintaining a constant airspeed, the student can control the altitude. If the airplane is climbing, a slight reduction of power can be made to remain in level flight. Further reductions in power will result in a descent, as shown in figure 5-4.

A practical application of the relationship of power and airspeed is made during the approach-to-landing phase of flight. If the airplane appears to be low and the resultant glide angle to be short while on final approach at a *constant*

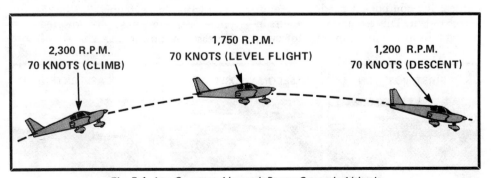

2,300 R.P.M.
70 KNOTS (CLIMB)

1,750 R.P.M.
70 KNOTS (LEVEL FLIGHT)

1,200 R.P.M.
70 KNOTS (DESCENT)

Fig. 5-4. At a Constant Airspeed, Power Controls Altitude

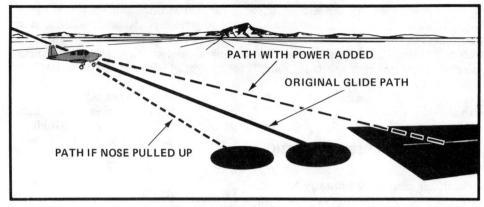

Fig. 5-5. Additional Power Extends Glide Path

airspeed, additional power must be applied to extend the glide path. As shown in figure 5-5, if control back pressure is applied in an attempt to maintain altitude, the airspeed decreases and an even steeper glide angle is created.

CLIMBS, DESCENTS, AND TURNS AT MINIMUM CONTROLLABLE AIRSPEED

As previously discussed, at a constant airspeed, altitude is controlled by power. To climb, the pilot adds power; to descend, he reduces power.

To execute turns at minimum controllable airspeed, the pilot must use a slightly different technique. As in any turn, part of the total lift force is diverted to make the airplane turn. For example, during a turn at normal cruise airspeed, the pilot must apply slight control back pressure to gain the extra vertical lift component needed to counteract weight. This requirement results in a slight decrease in airspeed. However,

during flight at minimum controllable airspeed, the loss of airspeed brings the airplane closer to the stall. The steeper the turn, the greater the load factor and the closer the airplane will be to the stall; therefore, power must be added to maintain airspeed and prevent the stall.

USE OF WING FLAPS

Maneuvering at minimum controllable airspeed also is practiced using extended flaps and landing gear, if the airplane has retractable gear. During practice, the pilot is instructed to lower the flaps a small amount at a time. At each position, he adjusts the attitude to maintain airspeed, adjusts power to maintain altitude, and adjusts trim to relieve control pressures.

Addition of flaps to the first position (10° to 15°) normally causes little pitch attitude, power, or trim change. However, with flaps extended 20° to 25°, the pitch attitude must be lowered. An increase in power and change of trim

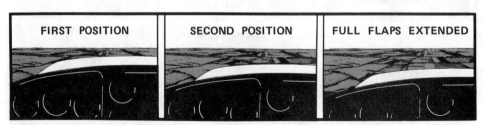

Fig. 5-6. Pitch Attitude Changes as Flaps Are Extended

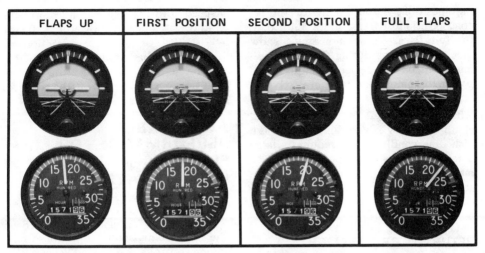

FLAPS UP	FIRST POSITION	SECOND POSITION	FULL FLAPS

Fig. 5-7. Pitch Attitude and Power Changes Required as Flaps Are Added

also are required. When the flaps are fully extended (about 40°), the pitch attitude change and power requirement usually are quite pronounced. The pitch attitude changes, as seen from inside the airplane, may follow the sequence shown in figure 5-6.

The attitude indications and tachometer settings associated with increasing flap extensions may look like those shown in figure 5-7. In this example, the required power settings to maintain level flight at 70 knots are 1,750 r.p.m. for slow flight with no flaps, 1,800 r.p.m. for the first

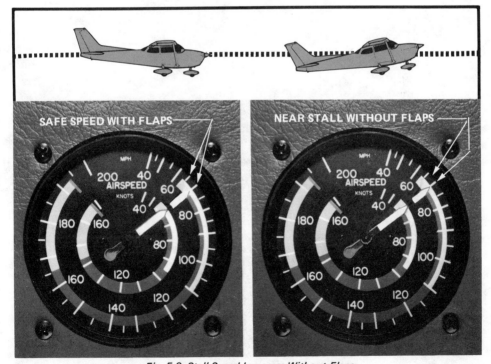

Fig. 5-8. Stall Speed Increases Without Flaps

flap position, 2,000 r.p.m. for the second position of flaps, and 2,300 r.p.m. for full flaps. These indications show that use of flaps during flight at minimum controllable airspeed requires added power to compensate for increased drag.

With the wing flaps fully extended, climb capability is very limited. This is a high drag condition and requires a large percentage of available power simply to maintain altitude. Full power will probably produce only a very slow rate of climb, if any.

RETURN TO CRUISE FLIGHT

To return to cruise airspeed from flight at minimum controllable airspeed, full power is applied first, a constant altitude is maintained with elevator, then the flaps are raised slowly, one position at a time. This technique is recommended to allow the speed to increase gradually as the flaps are retracted. In addition, while the airplane may have a safe margin of airspeed with the flaps extended, as seen on the left airspeed indicator in figure 5-8, sudden or complete retraction of the flaps at that speed may place the airplane near the stall speed in a no-flap condition, as shown by the airspeed indicator on the right.

ACCEPTABLE PERFORMANCE FOR FLIGHT AT MINIMUM CONTROLLABLE AIRSPEED

The pilot's performance is evaluated on the basis of his ability to establish minimum controllable airspeed, control the airplane positively, and recognize imminent stalls. Primary emphasis is placed on airspeed control. During straight-and-level flight at this speed, altitude should be maintained within 100 feet and heading within 10° of that assigned. Inadequate surveillance of the area prior to and during the maneuver or an unintentional stall is disqualifying.

SECTION B — POWER-OFF STALLS

Although stalls are practiced in an attempt to control airspeed, altitude, and attitude precisely, they are not practiced simply for the sake of stalling the airplane with perfection. Stalls are practiced to accomplish two main objectives. First, they enable the pilot to become familiar with the stall warnings and handling characteristics of an airplane as it transitions from cruise to slow flight and approaches the stall. This provides an awareness that a stall is imminent. Second, if the pilot inadvertently enters a stall, he will be able to recover promptly and effectively with a minimum loss of altitude.

CERTIFICATION REGULATIONS

FAR Part 23 prescribes the airworthiness standards for light airplanes used in flight training. It contains the regulations pertaining to flight performance and handling characteristics, structure, powerplant, equipment, and operating limitations.

Before a manufacturer can offer an airplane for sale, it must meet the specifications of this regulation, including flight testing and stall demonstrations. The airplane must meet the following specifications.

1. The pilot must be able to correct a roll or yaw up to the stall. This means that the pilot must have effective use of the controls up to actual stall occurrence.
2. The pilot must be able to prevent more than 15° of roll or 15° of yaw through normal use of controls during the recovery from a stall. In short, the controls must be effective during the recovery.
3. There must be a clear and distinct stall warning with the landing gear and flaps in any position the pilot chooses and in either straight or turning flight. The stall warning

must begin between 5 and 10 knots before the stall occurs, continue into the stall, and end with the recovery. The acceptable stall warning can be buffeting or vibration of the airplane just prior to the actual stall or a visual or aural stall warning instrument.
4. If the airplane loses more than 100 feet or pitches more than 30° nose-down during the stall demonstration, the information must be listed in the aircraft flight manual.

CAUSES OF THE STALL

Before stall practice begins, the factors which cause a stall should be reviewed. Simply stated, a stall is caused by an excessive angle of attack which causes the smooth air flow over the upper wing surface to break away, resulting in a loss of lift.

The angle of attack is the angle between the wing chord line and the direction that the wing is moving. Air moves toward the wing from the direction in which the wing is moving, or along the flight path of the airplane. This air flow is called relative wind. Therefore, the angle of attack is the angle between the wing chord line and the relative wind. (See Fig. 5-9.)

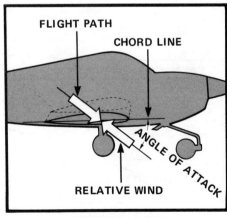

Fig. 5-9. Angle of Attack

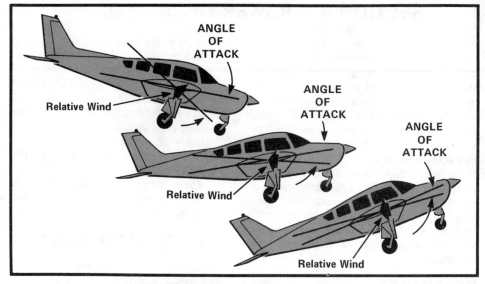

Fig. 5-10. Angle of Attack vs. Pitch Attitude

The wing can move through the air at several different angles with respect to the relative wind, as illustrated in figure 5-10. It is important to remember that the relative wind is seldom parallel to the horizon and that the angle of attack is measured between the chord line and relative wind, not the horizon. This means it is possible to have a high angle of attack with the nose low or a low angle of attack with the nose high.

In normal flight, the air flows over the top of the wing. However, even in cruise flight, the smooth air eventually separates from the wing at a certain point. This is called the separation point.

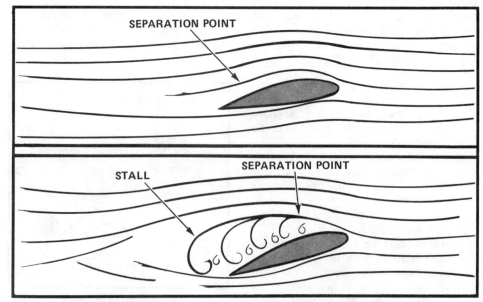

Fig. 5-11. Separation Point Moves Forward as Angle of Attack Increases

As the angle of attack increases, the separation point moves forward, as shown in figure 5-11. As the separation point moves forward, it eventually reaches a point where too much air has separated from the wing. There is no longer sufficient lift to support the airplane and the resulting drag has increased greatly, so the wings stall. It should be noted that all of the lift is not destroyed; however, the remaining lift is not sufficient to support the airplane.

FACTORS AFFECTING STALL SPEED

Code markings are used on the airspeed indicator to designate calibrated stall speeds in various configurations. For example, the stall speed in cruise configuration (wing flaps retracted and power off) can be read at the low speed end of the green arc. The stall speed in the landing configuration (wing flaps extended and power off) can be read at the low speed end of the white arc. (See Fig. 5-12.)

The stall speeds noted on the airspeed indicator are used as guide numbers only, since a smooth air flow separation point that causes a stall can be made to occur at faster airspeeds if the wing loading is increased. For example, the load factor can be increased by placing the airplane in a steep angle of bank while maintaining altitude. In straight-and-level flight, the load on the airplane is equal to the force of gravity (one G). In a level turn, as total lift increases to support the airplane, the centrifugal force and the effective load on the airplane increase. At a 60° angle of bank in *level flight*, both the total lift required to support the airplane and the load factor are doubled, as illustrated in figure 5-13.

The stall speed also is increased when the airplane is in a level turn. This increase is very small at shallow angles of bank. However, at a 45° angle of bank, the stall speed in most training airplanes increases by approximately 10 to 12 knots. At higher bank angles, the stall speed increases very rapidly. For example, at a 60° angle of bank, stall speed increases approximately 40 percent. In other words, an airplane that stalls at 55 knots in straight, unaccelerated flight will stall at 77 knots in a 60° bank.

As shown on the airspeed indicator, the extension of wing flaps also affects the stall speed. Flap extension increases the wing camber (curvature of wing) which allows the wings to produce sufficient lift to support the airplane at airspeeds slower than the flaps-up stall speed.

PRACTICE AREAS

Stalls should be practiced in an area away from other air traffic and at an altitude that generally permits stall recovery at least 1,500 feet above the ground. During stall practice, as well as in other maneuvers, the area must be

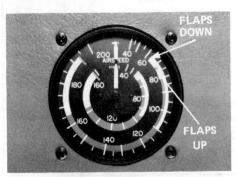

Fig. 5-12. Calibrated Stall Speeds

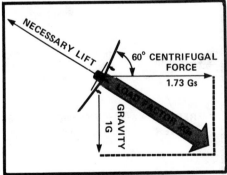

Fig. 5-13. Required Lift Increases With Angle of Bank

"cleared" of other airplanes. Clearing the area can be accomplished by making two 90° turns in opposite directions. However, the number of turns and in which direction really are not the important points. The object of the turns is to look over the entire area, especially at the flight altitude. The pilot should be sure that there are no other airplanes in the area. If there are airplanes nearby, the pilot should wait until they are well clear before performing the maneuver.

POWER-OFF STALLS

After a satisfactory altitude is established and the area has been cleared, the first stall usually is introduced from a power-off, wings-level glide, such as that used when landing the airplane. This is called a power-off stall.

To enter the stall, the pilot applies carburetor heat (if required), reduces power to idle, applies full flaps, establishes a normal glide, and trims the airplane. Next, he begins to slow the airplane by applying elevator or stabilator back pressure, as shown in figure 5-14.

As the airspeed slows, one objective of the maneuver is to gain a "feel" for the control pressures and responses as the airplane approaches the stall. As speed slows, the response of the airplane to control pressures becomes slower, and

greater displacement of the controls is necessary to achieve the desired results. The feeling is sometimes called "mushy" or "soft," as compared to the more solid feel of the controls at cruise speed. In addition, heavier control pressures are required to maintain the desired pitch attitude.

As the stall is approached, there are other cues that inform the pilot the airplane is slowing. For example, the tone and intensity of the slipstream noise and the changing engine sounds provide useful indications.

Stall warnings begin 5 to 10 knots before the stall. The warning indications may be a light, buzzer, horn, buffeting of the controls, or any combination of these. One of the purposes of stall practice is to recognize these indications, and the pilot must learn to recognize those applicable to his airplane.

During the first demonstration, the pilot will recover to straight-and-level flight *after* observing the stall warnings and before the stall is fully developed. Approaching close to the stall, but not fully stalling, is referred to as performing an imminent stall. The recovery should be initiated at the first indication of the stall by reducing the pitch attitude smoothly to decrease the angle of attack, as shown in figure 5-15.

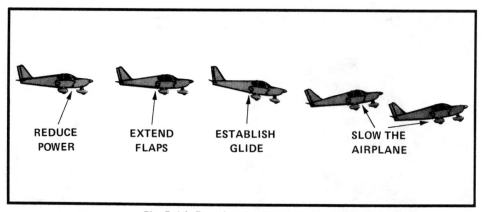

REDUCE POWER EXTEND FLAPS ESTABLISH GLIDE SLOW THE AIRPLANE

Fig. 5-14. Entering the Power-Off Stall

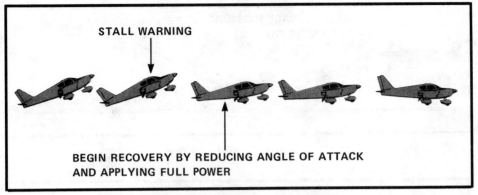

STALL WARNING

BEGIN RECOVERY BY REDUCING ANGLE OF ATTACK
AND APPLYING FULL POWER

Fig. 5-15. Recovery From an Imminent Stall

The pilot's first action is to decrease the angle of attack by releasing back pressure, while simultaneously applying power. The throttle is moved promptly and smoothly to obtain all available power, and appropriate rudder pressure is applied to center the ball of the turn coordinator to maintain coordinated flight. Care should be taken not to "jam" the throttle forward since this can cause the engine to falter. After the power is added, the carburetor heat control (if in use) is moved to the COLD position.

As the airplane accelerates in level flight, the flaps are retracted in accordance with the manufacturer's recommendations. Normally they are retracted to the takeoff position first, then as the speed increases, the remaining flaps are retracted gradually.

The object of stall recognition and recovery practice is to return the airplane to straight-and-level flight at cruise airspeed with a minimum loss of altitude. Coordinated, normal use of aileron and rudder is used to achieve this result. As airspeed increases following recovery, less right rudder pressure is required and power can be reduced to the normal cruise power setting.

FULL STALLS

After practicing imminent stalls, the pilot learns to recover from full stalls. The first part of full-stall practice requires exactly the same procedures as those required for imminent stalls. The warnings of the imminent stall are the same, but the angle of attack is increased *beyond* the point where recovery normally is initiated. Recovery is started *after* the nose pitches down, as shown in figure 5-16.

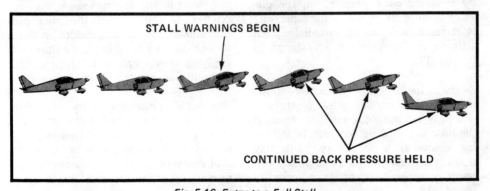

STALL WARNINGS BEGIN

CONTINUED BACK PRESSURE HELD

Fig. 5-16. Entry to a Full Stall

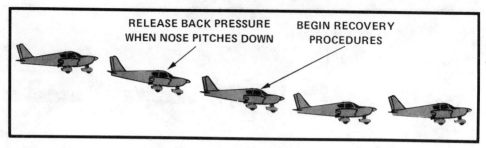

Fig. 5-17. Full-Stall Recovery

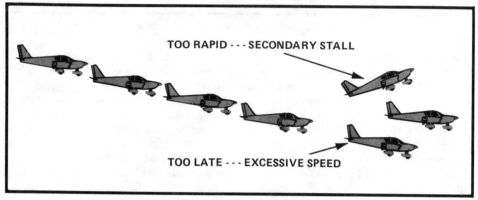

Fig. 5-18. Incorrect Full-Stall Recoveries

Fig 5-19. Coordination Aileron and Rudder Control Is Used During Stall Recovery

The pilot decreases the angle of attack by releasing back pressure on the elevator. The point at which back pressure is released and the approximate pitch attitude during recovery are shown in figure 5-17.

As the airspeed begins to increase following the recovery, the pilot gently and smoothly readjusts the pitch attitude. If the nose is pulled up too rapidly following recovery, a secondary stall may result. Conversely, a delayed pullup can result in excessive speed, as indicated in figure 5-18.

During full-stall practice, the airplane may tend to roll to one side as the nose pitches. If this occurs, the pilot uses coordinated aileron and rudder pressures to level the wings at the same time he is applying power and reestablishing pitch attitude, as illustrated in figure 5-19.

The same guidelines apply to power control as those learned during imminent stall recovery. The pilot applies power smoothly and promptly as he begins the stall recovery. Next, he uses normal flap retraction procedures as the airspeed increases.

ACCEPTABLE PERFORMANCE FOR POWER-OFF STALLS

The pilot is judged on his ability to recognize the indications of an imminent stall and take prompt, positive recovery actions. When practicing imminent stalls, he must not let a full stall develop. During full stall practice, he is expected to immediately recognize when the stall has occurred and take prompt, corrective action. The recovery must be performed without excessive airspeed, excessive altitude loss, a secondary stall, or loss of control, such as a spin.

SECTION C - STEEP TURNS

After proficiency is gained in the basic flight maneuvers, advanced maneuvers, such as steep turns, are introduced. Although steep turns are not required for FAA private pilot certification, the maneuver is excellent for developing coordination, planning, and precise airplane control. The commercial flight test, however, specifically requires right and left steep turns using a bank angle of at least 50°. The following discussion applies primarily to 45° bank steep turns, although the principles apply equally to the steeper turns required of the commercial pilot.

LIFT FORCE REQUIREMENTS

During a turn, the total lift force is diverted and part of the lift is used to make the airplane turn. When lift is diverted, the vertical component of lift used to support the airplane becomes insufficient and the airplane descends, unless action is taken to increase lift. (See Fig. 5-20.) Lift is increased and airspeed is decreased by increasing the angle of attack with back pressure on the control wheel.

In a 45° bank turn, the additional back pressure required and resulting loss of airspeed is more noticeable than in me-dium bank turns. In an airplane with a fixed pitch propeller, the decrease in airspeed also is accompanied by a decrease in r.p.m., with a resulting power loss. Consequently, more airspeed is lost in the attempt to maintain altitude.

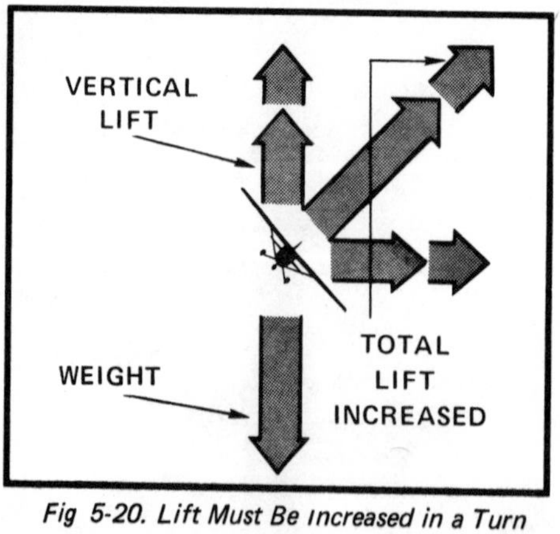

As the angle of bank is increased, stall speed increases and airspeed decreases as the pilot attempts to maintain altitude. This causes the stall speed and the airspeed to approach the same value. For example, if an airplane with a fixed pitch propeller normally stalls at 63 knots, it will stall at 90 knots in a 60° bank. If the airplane enters a 60° bank turn at its maneuvering speed of 110 knots and the airspeed drops to approximately 95 knots, the margin between airplane speed and stall speed is only five knots, as shown in figure 5-21.

STEEP TURN PROCEDURES

As in all training maneuvers, the pilot must be aware of other traffic within the area. Therefore, before beginning the maneuver, clearing turns should be made to insure the practice area is free of conflicting traffic. As the maneuver is performed, it is the pilot's responsibility to remain vigilant and avoid any traffic flying through the area.

Prior to entering steep turns, the pilot should stabilize the altitude, airspeed, and heading of the airplane. If the pilot begins the maneuver from a stabilized condition he can fly the maneuver more precisely. Section lines or prominent land features should be used to establish heading and aid in orientation.

TURN ENTRY

Steep turns are entered at the speed recommended by the airplane manufacturer. If no recommendation is listed,

VERTICAL LIFT

WEIGHT

TOTAL LIFT INCREASED

Fig 5-20. Lift Must Be Increased in a Turn

Fig. 5-21. Stall Speed and Airspeed Converge in Steep Turn

cruise speed or maneuvering speed, which-ever is lower, is used.

As the turn is entered, the bank should be established at a moderate rate and not rushed. If the airplane is rolled into the bank too rapidly, the pilot frequently encounters difficulty in establishing the pitch attitude to maintain level flight.

The normal procedure in an airplane with a fixed pitch propeller is to add power to maintain r.p.m. as the bank angle approaches 45°. Even with the application of power, there is an airspeed reduction and considerable back pressure must be applied. In many airplanes the trim tab can be used to help relieve pressure in the turn, but the pilot must remember that the trim must be changed again as soon as he rolls to level flight.

In an airplane with a constant speed propeller, power is normally at the cruise setting throughout the maneuver. However, the airspeed still decreases and con-trol wheel back pressure is required.

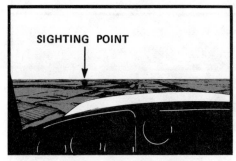

Fig. 5-22. Straight-And-Level Flight Pitch Attitude

Fig. 5-24. Pitch Attitude During a Steep Turn to the Right

VISUAL REFERENCES

The pitch attitude for straight-and-level flight at maneuvering speed is shown in figure 5-22. The sighting point above the nose of the airplane is approximately at the point of the arrow.

In figure 5-23, the airplane is established in a 45° steep bank turn to the left and is maintaining a constant altitude. The sighting point on the nose is higher than in straight-and-level flight due to the increased pitch attitude and angle of attack.

Figure 5-24 shows the airplane in a 45° steep bank turn to the right, also maintaining altitude. The most apparent difference is that, in a right turn, the nose seems to be considerably lower than in the left turn. However, the sighting point over the nose of the airplane is in the same position as in the turn to the left.

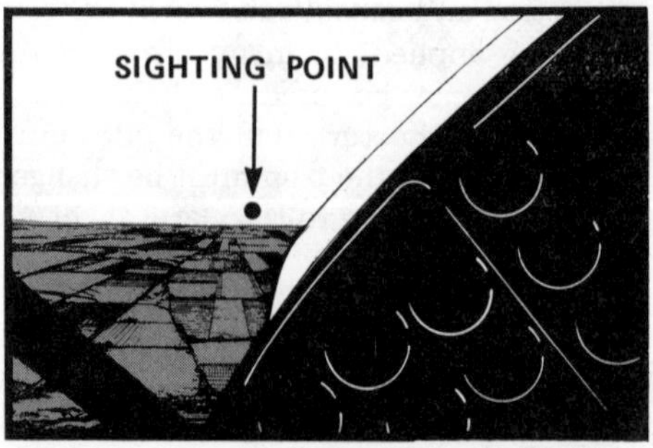

INSTRUMENT REFERENCES

During a 45° steep bank turn to the left using instrument references, the bank index shown in figure 5-25 indicates the number of degrees of bank. It should be noted that the nose of the miniature airplane is slightly above the horizon line, indicating a nose-high attitude.

During a 45° steep bank turn to the right, there is no change in the attitude references, except that the attitude indicator shows a bank to the right. The nose attitude is identical to the left turn indication, as shown in figure 5-26.

ALTITUDE CONTROL

In steep turns of 45° or more, altitude corrections deserve special consideration. If altitude is lost because of a nose-low attitude, simply pulling back on the control wheel is not a satisfactory cor-

Fig. 5-23. Pitch Attitude During a Steep Turn to the Left

Fig. 5-25. Instrument References During a Left, 45° Steep Bank Turn

Fig. 5-26. Instrument References During a Right, 45° Steep Bank Turn

rection. The force created by back pressure on the control wheel in a 45° bank raises the nose, but also tightens the turn. This procedure simply increases the load on the airplane and does little to correct for altitude. The proper response is to reduce the angle of bank temporarily and increase the pitch attitude simultaneously. When this correction has been made, the pilot then returns to the desired angle of bank and applies slightly more back pressure than previously used.

ROLL-OUT TECHNIQUE

The roll-out procedures for steep turns are performed in the same manner as those for medium bank turns; however, the roll-out should begin approximately 20° before reaching the desired heading. The pilot may notice a difference in the control pressures required during the roll-in and roll-out. Generally, less rudder pressure and aileron movement are required during the roll-in than during the roll-out because the control pressures exerted during the roll-out must overcome the airplane's over-banking tendency. This tendency is discussed later in this chapter.

The elevator or stabilator control pressures during roll-out are the reverse of those used during the roll-in. As the bank decreases, back pressure and pitch attitude must be decreased gradually to avoid gaining altitude, as indicated in figure 5-27.

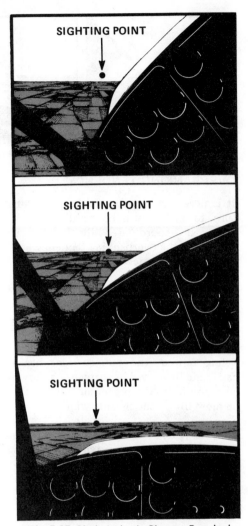

Fig. 5-27. Pitch Attitude Changes Required to Maintain Altitude

When proficiency is gained in normal steep bank turns, the pilot will learn to perform a steep turn in one direction, then in the other direction, with no hesitation between the turns. To accomplish this, the pilot rolls directly from one bank into the other, as illustrated in figure 5-28. This means back pressure is applied during the first turn, reduced during roll-out, then reapplied as the angle of bank increases in the opposite direction. Power changes also are coordinated with the pitch and bank attitude changes.

Fig. 5-28 Pitch Attitude Changes When Rolling From Left to Right Steep Turn

OVERBANKING TENDENCY

It is necessary to cross-control in a left turn to maintain a constant angle of bank and coordinated flight. This is caused by the overbanking tendency and is most pronounced at high angles of bank.

The overbanking tendency exists because when an airplane is in a steep turn, the wing on the outside of the turn travels farther than the inside wing. While traveling farther, the outside wing has a faster air flow over its surface. As shown in figure 5-29, the higher air flow results in more lift on the outside wing.

This increased lift tends to increase bank. To counteract this tendency, slight aileron pressure must be applied opposite to the turn to keep the airplane from overbanking.

At the same time, rudder pressure is required throughout the turn. The tail section, because of its distance aft of the center of gravity of the airplane, does not track in the same arc. (See Fig. 5-30.) Therefore, rudder pressure is needed to streamline the fuselage in the arc of the steep turn. The force needed to streamline the fuselage properly is greater than the amount required to counteract the aileron drag on the high wing. The use of cross-control technique keeps the airplane from overbanking and maintains coordinated flight, even though everything the pilot has learned to this point seems to contradict this.

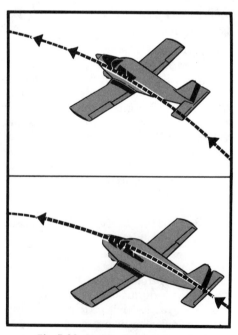

Fig. 5-30. Rudder Pressure Required During Steep Turn

TRAVELS
GREATER
DISTANCE →

LIFT

LIFT

TRAVELS
LESS
DISTANCE

Fig. 5-29. Overbanking Tendency

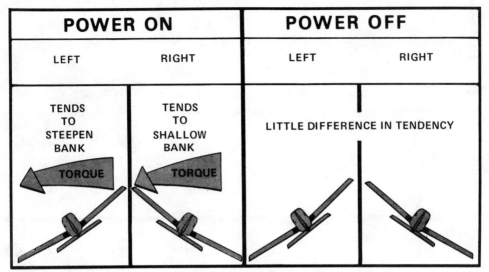

Fig. 5-31. Torque Affects Overbanking Tendency During Steep Turn

TORQUE AND P-FACTOR

Less overbanking tendency is evident in a right turn than in a left turn. This is due to torque and P-factor, which tend to roll the airplane to the left and work against the overbanking tendency in a right turn. However, these factors increase the overbanking tendency during left turns, as shown in figure 5-31.

ADJUSTMENTS DURING THE TURN

As in other types of turns, small adjustments must be made as the steep turn progresses. When the airplane is deviating from the desired attitude or altitude, the pilot should use the two-step method of stopping the deviation, then making small corrections back to the desired settings.

ACCEPTABLE PERFORMANCE FOR STEEP TURNS

Performance of steep turns is evaluated on the basis of planning, coordination, smoothness, prompt stabilization of turns, maintenance of constant bank and altitude, and orientation. The ability to roll from one turn directly into a turn in the opposite direction demonstrates the advanced coordination skills desired in this maneuver. All turn entries and recoveries should be accomplished promptly and smoothly, with appropriate power adjustments.

chapter 6

ADVANCED FLIGHT OPERATIONS

INTRODUCTION

As proficiency is gained in basic flight operations, the pilot is introduced to more advanced maneuvers and procedures. The advanced flight operations presented in this chapter include power-on and accelerated maneuver stalls, takeoffs and landings from unimproved fields, and emergency procedures. These maneuvers and procedures represent an important part of training because they relate directly to everyday flight operations. They also provide the pilot with an opportunity to advance his skill and proficiency significantly as he progresses toward private pilot certification.

SECTION A — POWER-ON AND ACCELERATED MANEUVER STALLS

Power-off stalls were discussed in Chapter 5. Once proficiency has been gained in power-off stalls, demonstration and practice of imminent and full stalls with power on are given.

An analysis of FAA accident statistics indicates that inadvertent stalls often result from lack of knowledge regarding the airplane's handling and performance characteristics during the takeoff and landing phases of flight. Therefore, one objective of practicing stalls and stall recoveries is to determine that the pilot can promptly recognize the control responses, kinesthetic sensations, and feel

of the airplane as it approaches a stall. A further objective is to enable him to make prompt, effective recoveries from both imminent and full stalls encountered in all normally anticipated flight situations.

POWER-ON STALLS

The power-on stall is the type most frequently encountered shortly after takeoff. This stall can occur if the pilot attempts to lift off and climb out at an airspeed below the normal takeoff speed or if he establishes an excessively high pitch attitude during the initial stage of the climbout.

The turning power-on stall normally occurs during the departure turn following take-off. This type of stall generally results from inattention. To simplify the discussion, these two types of stalls are discussed separately in this presentation.

STRAIGHT-AHEAD STALL

A power-on, straight-ahead stall may be encountered if the pilot attempts to lift the airplane from the runway at too slow an airspeed and applies excessive back pressure to the control wheel, producing an extremely nose-high attitude and high angle of attack. This type of stall also can occur when a pilot is flying at a low altitude over terrain which increases in elevation faster than the airplane is able to climb.

The recommended climb power setting, as specified by the airplane manufacturer, is used for stall practice. Although a high power setting is used during this stall, it should not be entered from a high airspeed. If a high airspeed is used, the pitch attitude encountered is extremely nose-high, resulting in an unrealistic stall situation, as shown in figure 6-1.

To prevent this excessive pitch attitude, power is reduced and the airplane slowed to liftoff speed while maintaining a constant altitude. Then, as liftoff speed is reached and back pressure is added to increase the angle of attack, power is increased simultaneously to the recommended climb power setting.

In order to maintain directional control and coordination, right rudder pressure is increased continually as the power and pitch attitude are increased. Throughout the approach to the stall and the recovery, a coordinated flight condition is maintained.

INDICATIONS OF THE APPROACHING STALL

As the airspeed is reduced, the pilot should develop an awareness of the various indications of the approaching stall. For example, the noise of the slipstream passing over the airplane decreases and the engine noise level decreases as the engine begins to labor during the climb. In addition, the flight controls develop an increasing mushiness or sluggish response. In contrast to the situation encountered in power-off stalls, the propeller slipstream causes the elevator and rudder controls to

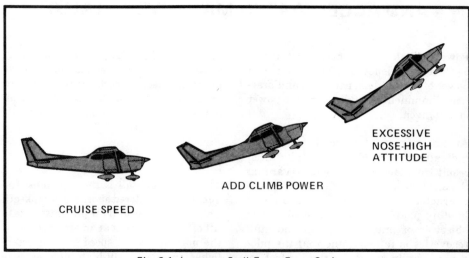

EXCESSIVE NOSE-HIGH ATTITUDE

ADD CLIMB POWER

CRUISE SPEED

Fig. 6-1. Improper Stall Entry From Cruise

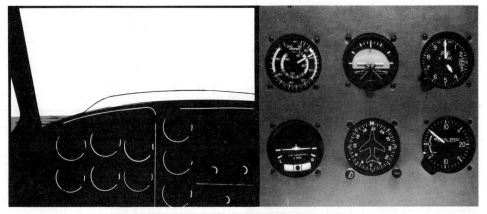

Fig. 6-2. Power-On Stall

be somewhat more effective and responsive than in the power-off stalls.

The pitch attitude in the power-on straight-ahead stall should resemble that

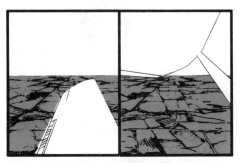

Fig. 6-3. High Angle of Attack

shown in the illustration in figure 6-2. The visual relationship of the nose and horizon are shown on the left and the instrument indications are pictured on the right. The angle created by the wingtips and the horizon also can provide a useful indication of the airplane's pitch attitude, as seen in figure 6-3.

RECOVERY PROCEDURES

The procedures for recovery from the stall are conventional. The angle of attack is *decreased*, full available power is applied simultaneously (if not already at full power), and coordinated aileron and rudder pressures are used to return the airplane to straight-and-level flight, as shown in figure 6-4.

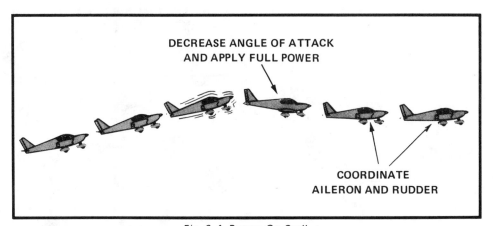

DECREASE ANGLE OF ATTACK
AND APPLY FULL POWER

COORDINATE
AILERON AND RUDDER

Fig. 6-4. Power-On Stall

FULL STALLS

After the pilot is familiar with the characteristics of the straight-ahead imminent stall, the stall warnings, and the changing control pressures, he begins practicing full stalls. This type of stall is entered in the same manner as the imminent straight-ahead stall. The area is cleared and power and airspeed reduced. As liftoff speed is attained, power is increased to the recommended climb power setting. The pilot should observe the indications of the approaching stall, maintain directional control, and continue to increase the angle of attack until the stall occurs. When the stall has developed fully, pronounced buffeting becomes evident and the nose pitches down, even though full back pressure is held. There is a tendency for the airplane to pitch more steeply and rapidly and exhibit more rolling tendencies to the right or left in the full stall than in the imminent stall.

To recover, the angle of attack is decreased by releasing elevator back pressure to lower the nose, as shown in figure 6-5. The rudder and ailerons are used in the normal coordinated manner to return the airplane to straight-and-level flight.

The prime consideration in effective stall recovery is minimum loss of altitude consistent with positive and effective control of the airplane. A common error during stall recovery is to use an excessive nose-down pitch attitude. However, the ideal recovery should be to a laterally level attitude that results in a minimum altitude loss and does not induce a secondary stall. In order to accomplish this, it is recommended that the airspeed not be permitted to exceed best angle-of-climb airspeed during the recovery.

TURNING STALLS

The power-on straight-ahead stall is a basic stall. The power-on turning stall is a variation of this basic stall.

Entry to a power-on turning stall is similar to that used for a straight-ahead stall, except a turn to the left or right is entered simultaneously. Recommended bank angles are from 15° to 20°. However, the airplane should not be allowed to vary between these bank angles. One specific angle should be selected and maintained until the stall occurs.

As the stall is approached, the angle of bank tends to steepen in a left turn and become shallower in a right turn because

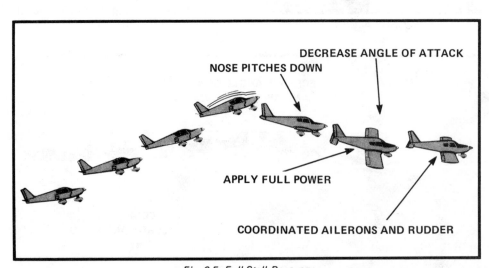

DECREASE ANGLE OF ATTACK

NOSE PITCHES DOWN

APPLY FULL POWER

COORDINATED AILERONS AND RUDDER

Fig. 6-5. Full-Stall Recovery

Fig. 6-6. Right-Turning Stall References

of the tendency of torque and P-factor to roll the airplane to the left. Each time the pilot practices stalls in each of these variations, he should strive to identify the indications of the approaching stall. The ailerons and rudder should be coordinated throughout the entire maneuver. Figure 6-6 illustrates the visual and instrument indications appropriate to the power-on right-turning stall.

To recover from a power-on turning stall, the airplane is returned to a straight-and-level attitude or slightly lower by using aileron and rudder pressure to level the wings. All available power is applied simultaneously.

The recovery is considered complete when the airplane regains straight-and-level flight. Figure 6-7 shows the visual and instrument indications during the recovery from the stall.

STALLS USING FLAPS

Stalls using flaps normally are practiced with partial flaps and with full flaps. Entry into the stall follows the normal procedures, except that flaps are lowered to the desired setting as the airplane slows. The stall can be practiced straight ahead or in moderate banks. As the stall is approached, aileron and rudder pressures are applied to assess the changing control responses.

Recovery is initiated when the imminent or full stall has developed. Procedures

Fig. 6-7. Stall Recovery References

are similar to those explained for other stalls. The angle of attack is decreased by releasing back pressure, while simultaneously applying all available power and using coordinated control pressures to level the wings.

One important difference in establishing the recovery pitch attitude when flaps are being used is that a more pronounced nose-down attitude is required during recovery. The increased nose-down attitude is required because the flaps add a significant amount of drag, resulting in a much slower rate of acceleration.

Stall recoveries with flaps are an important part of the training program, since flap extension and retraction procedures are generally performed close to the ground. If flaps are retracted rapidly without first allowing speed to build up, it is possible to induce a secondary stall or initiate a high rate of descent. However, during stall recoveries using *full* flap extension, it is generally recommended that the flaps be reduced to approximately one-third extension after the pitch attitude is reduced. In most light airplanes, this flap setting produces maximum lift and allows the airplane to accelerate more rapidly to a safe climb airspeed. The remainder of the flaps then can be retracted slowly after the airplane accelerates to at least the best angle-of-climb airspeed.

ACCELERATED MANEUVER STALLS

After practicing stalls with power on, power off, straight ahead, in turns, and with flaps up and down, the accelerated maneuver stall is introduced. The term *accelerated* is not related to the rapidity with which the stall is induced. Instead, it denotes a stall which occurs at a higher-than-normal airspeed because of the additional load factor which normally is induced during a steep turn or an abrupt increase in pitch attitude.

To avoid extremely high structural loads, accelerated maneuver stalls should not be performed at speeds more than 1.25 times the unaccelerated stall speed or with flaps extended. Abrupt pitch changes also should be avoided in airplanes with extensions between the engine and propeller because of the high gyroscopic loads produced. Since the load factor on the airplane increases anytime the airplane turns or the pitch attitude is increased, all of the stalls the pilot practices in turns with or without power are, to a degree, accelerated maneuver stalls. However, the stall speed increase is minimal.

The stall speed increase during an accelerated maneuver stall is approximately equal to the square root of the load factor. For example, if the airplane is placed in a 75° bank and level flight is maintained, a load factor of four Gs is imposed. Since the square root of four is two, the normal stall speed is multiplied by two to obtain the stall speed with the increased load factor. Assuming the airplane used in this example has a stall speed of 55 knots, in a 75° bank, the airplane will stall at the higher airspeed of 110 knots ($\sqrt{4} = 2 \times 55 = 110$).

Normally, a maximum load factor of 1.5 Gs is considered a limit for training purposes. A 45° to 50° angle of bank

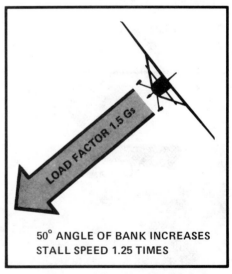

50° ANGLE OF BANK INCREASES STALL SPEED 1.25 TIMES

Fig. 6-8. Load Factor and Stall Speed

produces that load factor and increases the stall speed approximately 1.25 times the normal stall speed. Therefore, a 55-knot, unaccelerated stall speed increases to approximately 69 knots. (See Fig. 6-8.)

To begin an accelerated maneuver stall, the area is cleared of other air traffic through use of clearing turns. While in the latter part of a turn, the airplane is slowed to about 1.5 times normal stall speed and established in a 45° angle of bank while altitude is maintained. Then, the angle of attack is increased progressively by application of back pressure until the stall occurs. Five to seven knots above the new stall speed, the stall warning indications begin. At the time of the stall, pronounced buffeting occurs and the nose of the airplane is in an attitude similar to that illustrated in figure 6-9.

As with all stall practice, coordinated flight should be maintained during the entry and recovery. If the airplane is slipping to the inside of the turn at the time of the stall (the ball of the turn coordinator is to the inside of the turn), the upper wing tends to stall first and the airplane rolls rapidly to the outside

Fig. 6-9. Nose Position in Accelerated Maneuver Stall

of the turn. If the airplane is skidding to the outside of the turn (the ball is to the outside of the turn), the lower wing tends to stall first and the airplane rolls to the inside of the turn.

The recovery is initiated by releasing back pressure on the control wheel to reduce the angle of attack, while simultaneously adding full power. Aileron and rudder controls are used in a coordinated manner to level the wings and return to straight-and-level flight in the cruise condition, as shown in figure 6-10.

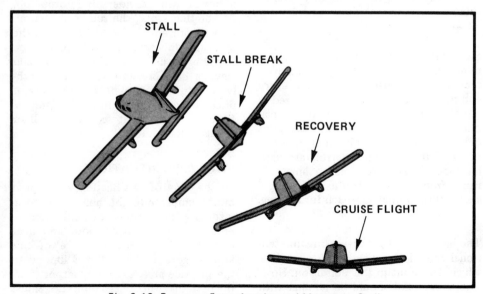

Fig. 6-10. Recovery From Accelerated Maneuver Stall

ACCEPTABLE PERFORMANCE FOR POWER-ON STALLS

The pilot's performance is judged on the basis of correct, prompt, and smooth use of control pressures to achieve the desired attitudes and prompt recognition of stall warnings. During performance of imminent stalls, he should initiate recovery before the nose pitches down. In recoveries from full stalls, there should be no evidence of secondary stalls or excessive descents.

SPINS

A spin is an aggravated stall which occurs when the airplane is in an uncoordinated flight condition. This results in a rotation about the airplane's vertical axis. During the rotation, the pitch attitude of the airplane can assume one of three positions—inverted, flat, or nose low. The inverted spin normally is not encountered unless the airplane is in inverted flight when the stall is entered. The flat spin can occur if the airplane is loaded near or beyond the aft center of gravity limit. The nose-low spin is the most frequently encountered; therefore, this discussion is based on that type of spin.

Since modern airplanes are designed to minimize the possibility of an inadvertent spin, demonstration of spin entry and recovery technique is not required as a part of the FAA private or commercial pilot flight test. However, each pilot must be aware that inadvertent spins can occur if the airplane controls are used improperly. For example, a spin can result from cross control usage during a stall or turn to final approach for landing.

The best method for preventing unintentional spins is to avoid flight situations which can result in this condition. However, every pilot should be familiar with basic spin recovery techniques.

NOTE:
Spin recovery techniques vary with airplane makes and models. If the correct procedure is not followed, the recovery may not be successful or the recovery time and the amount of altitude loss may be increased significantly. Therefore, the pilot must follow the procedure outlined by the airplane manufacturer for each airplane he flies. This procedure should be memorized so it is available for immediate recall. The following discussion pertains to a general recovery procedure. It is not intended to outline a technique for use in all types of airplanes.

As noted previously, the airplane must be in a stalled condition for a spin to occur. This stall must be broken before recovery can be initiated. To accomplish this in most airplanes, the elevator is positioned at or just forward of the neutral position, the ailerons are neutralized, and full rudder deflection is applied opposite the direction of spin rotation. If the direction of rotation is not readily apparent, the turn coordinator or turn indicator will provide this information. As rotation stops, the rudder is neutralized to prevent a secondary spin in the opposite direction. At this point, the airplane is in a straight descent and elevator back pressure is applied smoothly to return to level flight. The rate of pitch change also is controlled to prevent either an inadvertent secondary stall or excessive load forces.

STALL/SPIN SITUATIONS

At the time of certification, every pilot must demonstrate the ability to recognize the indications of and exercise prompt recovery from both imminent and full stalls. However, use of this knowledge and skill often is limited to the practice area, excluding airport traffic patterns where its application must be both timely and precise. Two infrequent, but hazardous, stall/spin situations are discussed in the following paragraphs.

IMMEDIATELY AFTER TAKEOFF

A stall may occur immediately after takeoff from an airfield which is too short for the planned operation. A combination of a short runway and obstacles in the departure path may encourage the pilot to maintain an excessively high pitch attitude which reduces the climb rate and causes the airplane to stall.

This situation can be avoided by planning the departure carefully. The actual takeoff requirements are determined from airplane performance charts, then adapted to local weather conditions, airport surface conditions, and pilot skills. These calculations are compared to the available runway lengths and obstacle clearance needs so the pilot can gauge actual airplane performance and determine the proper climb airspeeds and airplane configurations.

DURING TURN TO FINAL APPROACH

Many stall/spin mishaps occur during the turn from base leg to final approach. This situation may develop when a strong quartering crosswind drifts the airplane downwind and toward the landing runway. Consequently, the pilot may increase the bank attitude to tighten the turn without applying sufficient coordinated rudder pressure. At the same time the load factor is increased. This action results in an increased stall speed and an altitude loss. If the pilot raises the nose in an attempt to conserve altitude, the stage is set for a cross-control, stall/spin.

To avoid this situation, the turn to final approach should be initiated sooner. This technique eliminates the need for a steep bank during the turn and facilitates a stabilized final approach.

LIMITATIONS

Another important consideration in regard to spins is aircraft limitations. Airplanes are categorized according to their intended use and operating limitations. Airplane categories include transport, normal, utility, acrobatic, and restricted. Many airplanes used in training activities often are certified in both the normal and utility categories. Utility category aircraft typically are certified for limited acrobatic maneuvers. For example, maneuvers involving more than 60° of bank, including steep turns, chandelles, lazy eights, and spins may be approved, provided the airplane is operated according to the applicable utility category limitations. These limits usually consist of a lower maximum takeoff weight and/or a smaller CG range. The aft CG limit usually is located forward of the limit approved for normal category operations; and other loading restrictions commonly apply to the utility category.

When a normal/utility airplane is operated according to the limitations of the normal category, certain maneuvers normally are prohibited. For instance, acrobatics, spins, or spins with flaps extended may not be authorized. All of these limitations are listed in the pilot's operating handbook, approved flight manual, and/or indicated by specific markings and placards.

In addition, certain regulations may apply to a given category of airplane. As an example, a restricted category airplane is prohibited from flight over a densely populated area. From this discussion, it is apparent that pilots need to know the specific limitations and regulations that apply to their airplane category. Maneuver limitations, such as spins, are particularly significant. *If an airplane is not certified for spinning, there is no assurance that recovery from a spin in that airplane is possible.*

SECTION B – MAXIMUM PERFORMANCE TAKEOFFS AND LANDINGS

The next procedures and techniques to be introduced and practiced are maximum performance takeoffs and landings. These maneuvers include short-field and soft-field takeoffs and landings.

TERMINOLOGY

Before practicing maximum performance takeoffs, the pilot must understand the difference between *best angle-of-climb airspeed* and *best rate-of-climb airspeed*. The best angle of climb provides the greatest altitude gain in the *shortest distance* traveled, while the best rate of climb provides the greatest altitude gain in the *shortest time*. Since the objective of the short-field takeoff is to gain the maximum altitude in the minimum distance, the best angle-of-climb is used for this procedure.

SHORT-FIELD TAKEOFF AND MAXIMUM CLIMB PERFORMANCE

During short-field practice sessions, it usually is assumed that, in addition to a short runway, there is an obstruction on each end of the runway that must be cleared. The obstruction is considered to be approximately 50 feet in height, as illustrated in figure 6-11.

The pretakeoff checklist is the same as that used for normal takeoff procedures, except that flaps are set as recommended by the airplane manufacturer to achieve a maximum performance climb. The recommended flap setting varies between airplanes and can range from no flaps to two-thirds flaps.

The short-field takeoff should be initiated by holding the brakes, applying full power, and then releasing the brakes. This procedure does not necessarily shorten the total takeoff ground run, but it enables the pilot to determine that the engine is functioning properly before taking off from a field where power availability is critical. A running, turning takeoff is not recommended, especially at high speeds, because this technique does not permit stabilization of fuel level in the tanks of some makes and models of airplanes.

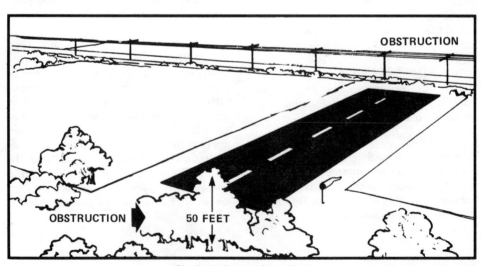

OBSTRUCTION

OBSTRUCTION　50 FEET

Fig. 6-11. Typical Short Field

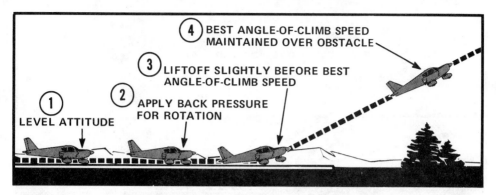

Fig. 6-12. Rotation and Liftoff During Short-Field Takeoff

Directional control is maintained with rudder pressure. The airplane should be allowed to roll on the full weight of its wheels in an attitude that results in minimum drag, as shown in figure 6-12, position 1.

The initial takeoff roll involves little or no use of elevator or stabilator control beyond permitting it to assume a neutral position. Shortly before the best angle-of-climb airspeed is reached (position 2), back pressure is applied smoothly and promptly so that the airplane lifts off near the best angle-of-climb speed (position 3). This attitude and airspeed are held until the obstacle is cleared (position 4). Caution should be taken to avoid raising the nose too soon. A premature nose-high attitude during the takeoff ground run produces more drag and causes a longer takeoff roll.

After the obstacle has been cleared, the airplane is adjusted to the normal climb attitude. If flaps are used, they should be retracted only after the obstacle is cleared and the best rate-of-climb speed is established. Flap retraction completes the short-field takeoff procedure and normal climbout, power adjustment, and leveloff procedures are resumed.

ACCEPTABLE PERFORMANCE FOR SHORT-FIELD TAKEOFFS

The pilot's performance is evaluated on the basis of planning, smoothness, direc-

tional control, and accuracy. In simulating a short-field takeoff, the liftoff and climb should be performed within five knots of the best angle-of-climb speed.

SHORT-FIELD LANDING

During a short-field landing it is assumed the approach and landing are made over a 50-foot obstacle. The landing is performed from a full flap, stabilized power approach with the touchdown executed with power-off at minimum controllable airspeed. By incorporating this technique, the airplane can be maneuvered safely and accurately over the obstacle to a landing touchdown at the slowest possible groundspeed, producing the shortest possible ground roll.

The early part of the approach on the downwind leg and through the turn to base leg is very similar to a normal approach. The pilot may extend one-third of the available flaps during the latter portion of the downwind leg, two-thirds on base, and the remaining flaps on final approach while progressively reducing the airspeed. This enables the pilot to make the transition to short-field approach speed in smooth, easy steps. During the transition, the trim tab should be used to remove control pressure.

FINAL APPROACH

When the airplane is aligned with the runway centerline, the remaining flaps

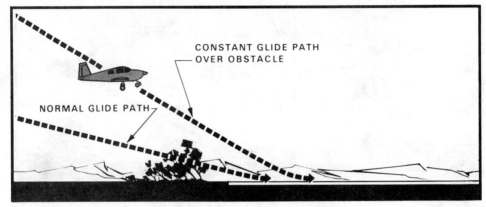

Fig. 6-13. Approach Angle Comparison

are extended and the airspeed established at the speed recommended by the airplane manufacturer. During the final approach, it is vital that a constant glide angle is maintained over the obstacle until the landing flare is initiated, as indicated in figure 6-13. To achieve a constant glide angle, a stabilized power approach at a constant airspeed and constant rate of descent is established. Since the approach to landing is slightly higher than normal with a steeper glide path, it is important to establish the descent profile early in the approach. Once the airspeed is established, it must remain constant with small power corrections, as necessary.

If the pilot discovers the airplane is slightly low on the approach and applies back pressure to decrease the rate of descent, the airspeed also decreases. When the airspeed decreases, the groundspeed decreases. Figure 6-14 shows that if the groundspeed decreases, the distance of forward travel also decreases. Both airplanes in this example are descending at 400 feet per minute, but have different groundspeeds. At the end of one minute, both airplanes will have descended 400 feet, but the airplane on glide path 1 will have traveled 1.06 miles forward, while the airplane on glide path 2 will have a forward travel of only 0.93 miles. The mileage differential between the two approaches represents approximately 790 feet; therefore, application of back pressure does not ultimately affect the rate of descent, only the distance of forward travel.

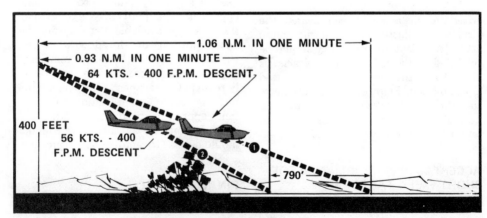

Fig. 6-14. Glide Path Comparison

LANDING FLARE AND TOUCHDOWN

During the landing flare, power is reduced smoothly to idle and the airplane is allowed to touch down in a full-stall attitude. When the airplane is firmly on the runway, the brakes can be applied, as necessary, to further shorten the landing roll. However, the flaps should be retracted prior to brake application to increase the weight on the main gear and increase the braking action.

ACCEPTABLE PERFORMANCE FOR SHORT-FIELD LANDINGS

The pilot's performance is evaluated on the basis of his planning, coordination, smoothness, and accuracy. He must control the angle of descent and airspeed on final approach so that floating is minimized during the flare. After touchdown, he must bring the airplane to a stop smoothly, within the shortest possible distance consistent with safety.

SOFT-FIELD TAKEOFF

The objective of the soft-field takeoff is to transfer the weight of the airplane from the main landing gear to the wings as quickly and smoothly as possible. The soft-field takeoff procedure requires accelerating the airplane in a nose-high attitude with the nosewheel clear of the surface during most of the takeoff ground run, as shown in figure 6-15. This technique keeps the nosewheel from sinking into the soft runway surface and allows the airplane to accelerate to lift-off speed. If the pitch attitude is established properly during the ground run, the airplane will lift off at or slightly below the power-off stall speed. After liftoff, the pitch attitude is reduced gradually to level flight, allowing the airplane to accelerate within ground effect to the normal climb airspeed.

PRETAKEOFF CONSIDERATIONS

The soft-field takeoff procedure actually begins during the taxi phase of the operation. If the taxi area is soft, certain taxi procedures must be used prior to the actual takeoff. The pilot should be aware that full-up elevator or stabilator deflection with a slight amount of power helps keep the airplane moving in soft-field conditions. This technique transfers some of the weight of the airplane from the nosewheel to the main wheels, resulting in lower power requirements and greater ease in taxiing. After the pretakeoff checklist is complete, the flaps are extended to the setting specified by the manufacturer.

The approach area and traffic pattern are cleared prior to taxiing onto the takeoff area. In this manner, when there is no conflicting traffic, the airplane can be transitioned from the taxi phase to the takeoff roll without stopping. This technique allows the airplane to maintain momentum and ultimately decreases the total takeoff distance.

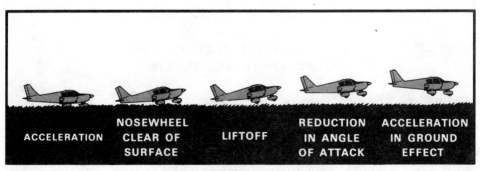

| ACCELERATION | NOSEWHEEL CLEAR OF SURFACE | LIFTOFF | REDUCTION IN ANGLE OF ATTACK | ACCELERATION IN GROUND EFFECT |

Fig. 6-15. Soft-Field Takeoff

USE OF RUDDER

As the airplane is taxied into position for takeoff and aligned properly with the runway centerline, the remaining power is applied smoothly and the elevator or stabilator back pressure maintained. With the application of takeoff power, right rudder pressure is required to maintain directional control due to the effects of torque, P-factor, and spiraling slipstream. As the weight on the nosewheel is eliminated, nosewheel steering becomes ineffective. However, due to the slipstream flow, use of the rudder is adequate for maintaining directional control.

PITCH CONTROL

As power is applied and the takeoff roll is initiated, full elevator or stabilator back pressure is applied to raise the nosewheel from the soft runway surface. As the speed increases and the elevator or stabilator becomes more effective, a slight reduction in back pressure is required to maintain the necessary constant pitch attitude. If the back pressure is not reduced, the airplane may assume an extremely nose-high attitude which, in some airplanes, can cause the tail skid to come in contact with the runway or cause a premature liftoff.

LIFTOFF AND FLAP RETRACTION

The liftoff should be accomplished at or slightly before reaching the power-off stall speed in the landing configuration. As the airplane lifts from the runway surface, a further reduction in back pressure must be initiated to achieve a

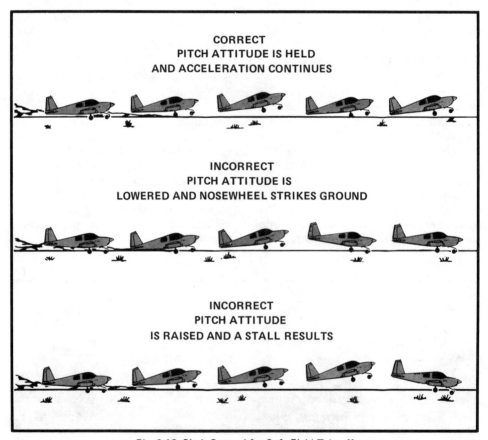

Fig. 6-16. Pitch Control for Soft-Field Takeoff

level flight attitude. The airplane then must be accelerated in level flight, within ground effect, to the best angle-of-climb airspeed before the flaps are retracted. If the flaps are retracted prematurely, the resultant loss in lift may cause the airplane to settle back onto the runway.

On a rough surface, it is possible for the airplane to skip or bounce into the air before the full weight of the airplane can be supported aerodynamically. Therefore, it is important for the pilot to hold the pitch attitude as constant as possible (an important application of flight at minimum controllable airspeed), as shown in the top portion of figure 6-16. If the airplane settles back to the surface, it can continue its acceleration to takeoff speed. Permitting the nose to lower after a bounce may cause the nosewheel to strike the ground with resulting damage, as shown in the middle portion of figure 6-16. On the other hand, sharply increasing the pitch attitude after a bounce may cause the airplane to stall, as shown in the bottom portion of the illustration.

GROUND EFFECT

Ground effect is a temporary gain in lift during flight at very low altitudes. It is due primarily to the compression of the air between the wings of the airplane and the ground. In part, ground effect also is influenced by wingtip vortices, as shown in figure 6-17. Ground effect allows the airplane to sustain flight at very low airspeeds and altitudes. However, this phenomenon is limited to a height above the ground which is about equal to the airplane's wingspan. For example, if the wingspan of the airplane is 40 feet, ground effect terminates at approximately 40 feet above ground level, as shown in figure 6-18. Since the intensity of ground effect decreases with altitude, the airplane should be flown as low as safety will permit until the best angle-of-climb airspeed is achieved.

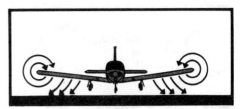

Fig. 6-17. Ground Effect

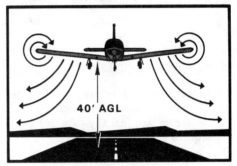

40' AGL

Fig. 6-18. Ground Effect Diminishes
With Altitude

OBSERVATION OF PROPER AIRSPEEDS

Throughout the takeoff procedure, the proper airspeeds must be observed and the necessary climb segments planned accordingly. After the airplane is airborne, the best angle-of-climb speed is achieved as quickly as possible. At this point, the pilot may begin to retract the flaps slowly. Flap retraction increases the rate of acceleration to the best rate-of-climb airspeed. When this airspeed is reached, the pilot may begin a normal climb and retract any remaining flaps. Then, the pilot can transition the airplane smoothly to an enroute climb airspeed, if appropriate. The enroute climb airspeed provides increased visibility over the nose of the airplane during the climb to the cruising altitude.

ACCEPTABLE PERFORMANCE FOR SOFT-FIELD TAKEOFFS

The pilot's performance is evaluated on the basis of his planning, directional control, smoothness, and accuracy. He must lift the airplane off at a speed not higher

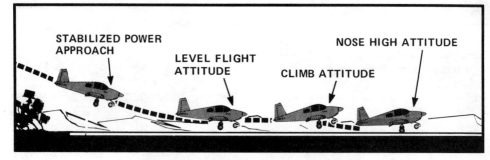

Fig. 6-19. Soft-Field Landing With Full Flaps

than the power-off stall speed and observe normal climbout speed.

The most frequent errors are improper pitch, rudder, and airspeed control. These errors are usually the result of inadequate planning.

SOFT-FIELD LANDING

The soft-field landing is conducted from a normal full-flap approach and the landing touchdown is executed with a high angle of attack while applying necessary power for a soft touchdown. The objective is to ease the weight of the airplane from the wings to the main wheels as gently and slowly as possible. If the landing is executed properly, the total weight of the airplane rests on the main wheels with the nosewheel free of the soft surface during most of the landing roll, as shown in figure 6-19. This landing technique prevents the nosewheel from sinking into the soft surface and reduces the possibility of an abrupt stop during the landing roll.

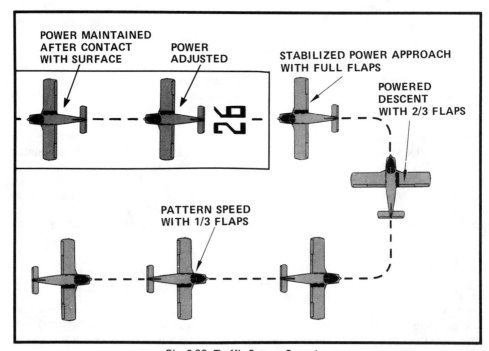

Fig. 6-20. Traffic Pattern Procedure

TRAFFIC PATTERN AND USE OF FLAPS

Planning for the soft-field landing begins in the traffic pattern, as shown in figure 6-20. Preparation for the landing should be initiated on the downwind leg where the airplane is transitioned from cruise to pattern speed with one-third flaps extended. On the base leg, two-thirds flaps are added and, on final approach, full flaps are applied. At this point, a stabilized power approach is executed, with emphasis upon a uniform rate of descent and constant glide angle.

PITCH AND POWER CONTROL DURING LANDING

Proper pitch and power control are important during the entire approach and landing, but become most critical during the landing flare and touchdown segments. The pitch must be transitioned smoothly from an approach attitude, through level flight, to a climb attitude which allows touchdown on the main wheels. Normally, a small amount of power is maintained during the touch-down to facilitate the continuous angle of attack with the nosewheel clear of the soft runway surface during the touch-down and roll-out. The amount of power required varies with gross weight and density altitude. When power is maintained, the slipstream flow over the empennage makes the elevator or stabilator more effective. If power is reduced, the air flow is too slow for elevator or stabilator effectiveness and back pressure does not produce the desired result. As the airspeed decreases on the roll-out, the slipstream becomes less effective and the nosewheel contacts the soft surface gradually and smoothly, without a change in power setting.

ACCEPTABLE PERFORMANCE FOR SOFT-FIELD LANDINGS

The pilot's performance is evaluated on the basis of his planning, smoothness, and accuracy. He must maintain the final approach airspeed within five knots of that prescribed. If the flaps are retracted during the landing roll, the pilot must exercise extreme caution and maintain positive control.

SECTION C - EMERGENCY LANDING PROCEDURES

Since modern airplane engines are extremely reliable, actual mechanical malfunctions are rare. However, inadvertent fuel starvation or an actual engine component malfunction may require the pilot to make an emergency landing. Five general steps used to cope with this type of situation are listed in sequence.

1. Establish the best glide speed.
2. Scan the immediate area for a suitable field.
3. Turn to a heading that will take the airplane to that field.
4. Attempt to determine the cause of the power failure and restart the engine, if possible.
5. Set up a landing approach to the selected field.

ESTABLISHING ATTITUDE AND GLIDE SPEED

If the engine fails, the pilot should attempt to conserve altitude by application of back pressure on the control wheel as the airplane is slowed to the best glide speed. This speed is normally specified by the airplane manufacturer and is usually close to the approach speed without flaps.

As the best glide speed is attained, the airplane is trimmed to relieve the control pressures and to aid in maintaining the proper attitude and airspeed. If the airspeed is below the best glide speed at the time of power failure, the nose is lowered immediately to the best glide attitude and the airplane is retrimmed. If the flaps are extended, the airspeed is increased to a safe flap retraction speed, the flaps retracted, the proper attitude established, and the airplane retrimmed.

SELECTING A FIELD

A field should be selected within the immediate area. As a general guideline,

the pilot should select a field that can be evaluated easily for obstructions and terrain, and one that is within gliding distance from the present altitude. The pilot who selects a field several miles from his present position and arrives to find it covered with rocks and trees and crisscrossed with several ditches or fences would have been better off to have selected a field within the immediate area over which he was flying.

Experience and familiarity with the general terrain in the training area help in the selection of the field. However, there are many variables to consider, including the wind direction and speed, length of the field, obstructions, and the surface condition. These various factors must be evaluated and a decision made concerning the field that provides the greatest possibility of a successful landing.

A long field lying into the wind with a firm, smooth surface that is free of obstructions is the most desirable. However, all of these features are seldom available. On one occasion, it may be better to accept a crosswind landing on a long field, rather than attempt to land into the wind on a very short field. On another occasion, a downwind landing with light winds and no obstructions may be preferable to a landing into the wind with numerous obstructions.

MANEUVERING

If the previous suggestions are followed, the selected field should be within easy gliding distance. This means that the airplane should be headed directly for the field and any excess altitude should be dissipated near the selected field. From that vantage point, the pilot is in a good position to observe the field carefully for wires, fences, holes, tree stumps, ditches, or other hazards that were not observed easily from a greater distance.

It is inadvisable to circle away from the field, then try to make a long, straight-in glide to the field. The estimation of glide distance from a faraway point is difficult even for experienced pilots. A circling approach over the field allows the pilot to make adjustments for altitude and keeps him in a position from which he can reach the field.

DETERMINING CAUSE OF FAILURE

When the glide is set up, the field selected, and the airplane headed for that field, the pilot should attempt to find the cause of the malfunction and restart the engine. Sudden engine power loss normally is caused by a fuel problem; therefore, the pilot should check to make sure the fuel selector is on and is set to a tank that has fuel.

Next, the mixture is checked to see that it is in the RICH position and the auxiliary fuel pump is turned on, if the airplane is so equipped. Carburetor heat also should be applied early in the procedure to determine if ice has formed and attempt to remove it. Then the magneto switch should be checked to see that it is in the BOTH position. If the cause of the power failure cannot be

determined, the pilot should scan other instruments and make a general inspection inside the cabin to obtain some indication of the cause of the failure.

The pilot should be methodical, perform his checks in a definite sequence, and take time to be thorough with the cabin check. It may seem as though it takes minutes to accomplish this, but it requires only a few seconds to make an unhurried check. If the cause of the power failure is discovered and remedied, engine restarting does not require use of the starter, since the propeller continues to turn, or windmill, in a power-off glide.

EMERGENCY LANDING APPROACH

180° SIDE APPROACH

Ideal planning should place the airplane at the 180° point when normal traffic pattern altitude is reached, as shown in figure 6-21. From that point, the approach is like a normal power-off approach to an airport. The pilot should be able to use all of the normal cues to turn base leg, judge position, and turn to final. The value of this procedure is that it places the pilot in a position where he

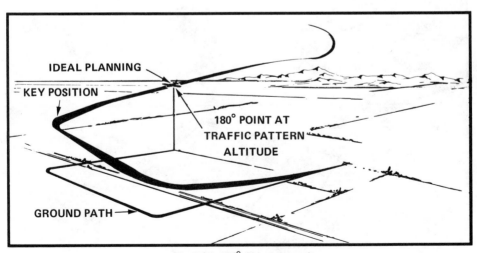

Fig. 6-21. 180° Side Approach

has familiar points from which to make judgments on glide angle, speed, and distances.

Unfortunately, it is not always possible to reach the ideal position. The pilot may have to use a right-hand pattern instead of a left-hand pattern because of his position. If the altitude at which power failure occurs is too low or the distance to a suitable landing field is too great, the pilot may not be able to arrive at either a left or a right 180° position. If this situation occurs, the alternative is to plan the approach so that the airplane can intercept the normal traffic pattern. For example, the next best place for interception may be the key position, as illustrated in figure 6-22. The pilot should try to visualize a normal traffic pattern overlying the chosen field, then consider the altitude and his position so he can plan to intercept the traffic pattern at the earliest point.

Flaps should be used as required during the approach. It is recommended that full flaps be used only after the turn to final is completed and the pilot is assured of reaching the intended field.

During emergency landings, the pilot must remember the distance traveled in the landing flare because the glide angle aiming point is short of the actual touchdown point. For example, figure 6-23 shows the desired landing point just beyond a ditch. In this situation, the aiming point must be on the near side of the ditch. When the approach is executed properly, it will appear that the airplane will touch down short of the intended point, as illustrated in figure 6-24. During the flare, however, the airplane will glide across the ditch and land at the desired spot, as shown in figure 6-25.

GO-AROUNDS

If the selected field is an approved landing area, the instructor may require the student to proceed and land. If the field is not approved, a go-around should

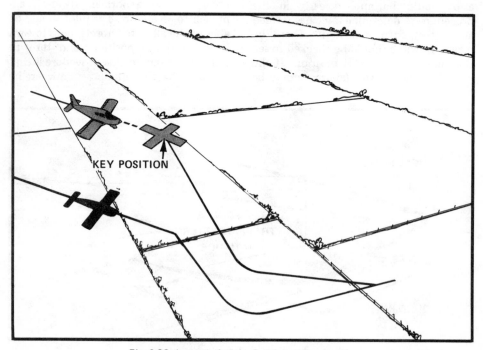

KEY POSITION

Fig. 6-22. Intercepting the Pattern at Key Position

Fig. 6-23. Final Approach for Emergency Landing

Fig. 6-24. Aiming and Touchdown Point

Fig. 6-25. Flare and Touchdown

be initiated when the instructor specifies. The altitude for the go-around should be low enough that it is apparent whether or not the outcome of the simulated emergency landing would have been successful.

Both the instructor and the student should understand who will perform the go-around. If the instructor specifies that he will take control of the airplane, the student should relinquish control completely. When the instructor has assumed control, the student should not touch the flight controls, retract flaps, or perform any other function unless directed to do so.

To initiate the go-around, all available power is applied, carburetor heat is placed in the COLD position, and the airspeed is established at or above the best angle-of-climb speed before flap retraction is initiated. When well clear of all obstructions, a normal climb is resumed. In order to conform with normal traffic pattern procedures, no turns are recommended below 400 feet AGL.

EMERGENCY LANDING PRACTICE

Since most practice emergency landing approaches terminate in a go-around, it is possible for the pilot to fall into the habit of considering the procedure as just another training exercise. To avoid this, it should be assumed that each simulated emergency landing will actually result in a landing. Careful cultivation of this assumption prepares the pilot for the possibility that he may be required to perform an actual emergency landing.

As a final note, emergency landing practice puts the airplane in a precarious position in the event of unforseen circumstances. For this reason, these procedures should be practiced *only* when the instructor is in the airplane.

PARTIAL POWER MALFUNCTIONS

In addition to emergency landing practice, the pilot must know how to cope with certain other situations. To practice these procedures, the instructor simulates or states a given problem, then demonstrates or explains the appropriate corrective actions. These problems may include partial loss of power, rough engine operation, carburetor ice, fuel starvation, and fire in the engine compartment.

OTHER EMERGENCY PROCEDURES

In addition to partial or complete power malfunctions, the pilot should become familiar with other system or equipment malfunctions. These should include inoperative electrical system, electrical fire or smoke in the cabin, gear or flap malfunctions, door opening in flight, and inoperative elevator trim tab. The pilot also should be familiar with the proper course of action in the event he becomes lost, trapped on top of an overcast, loses radio communications, or encounters unanticipated adverse weather.

ACCEPTABLE PERFORMANCE FOR EMERGENCY PROCEDURES

Performance of emergency procedures is evaluated on the basis of the pilot's prompt analysis of the situation and his remedial course of action. He must perform the emergency procedures in compliance with the manufacturer's published recommendations. Any action which creates unnecessary additional hazards is disqualifying.

chapter 7

INTRODUCTION

Attitude instrument flying is a fundamental method for controlling an airplane by reference to instruments. It is based on an understanding of the flight instruments and systems and the development of the skills required to interpret and translate the information presented by the instruments into precise airplane control. Instrument cross-check, instrument interpretation, and airplane control are the three fundamental skills involved in all instrument flight maneuvers. These skills may be developed individually, then integrated into the unified, smooth, positive control responses required to maintain any prescribed flight path.

The basic elements of attitude instrument flying are not presented to qualify the noninstrument rated pilot to fly in instrument conditions. Instrument training is required for private pilot certification to enable the pilot to extricate himself from a hazardous encounter with IFR weather conditions. Even after the pilot has attained reasonable skill in performing the basic attitude instrument maneuvers and recoveries from critical attitudes, he should never undertake flight in instrument conditions. However, these newly acquired skills will serve as a firm foundation for further instrument training and the eventual acquisition of an instrument rating.

FLIGHT INSTRUMENTS

In visual flight, airplane attitude usually is determined by reference to the earth's horizon. For example, pitch attitude normally is determined by the position of the airplane's nose in relation to the natural horizon, while the wingtips provide information concerning bank. However, when flying in visual conditions, the airplane's attitude is not determined by looking down at the ground and estimating the height, but by reference to the altimeter. The speed of the airplane can be approximated by the sound of the slipstream, but it is determined more precisely through use of the airspeed indicator. The direction of flight can be approximated in relation to the sun's position, but it is easier to use the heading indicator.

Flight by instrument references, therefore, utilizes the same information as gained from the instruments in visual flying. However, the *attitude indicator* plays a predominant role during instrument flight. This instrument becomes the substitute for the natural horizon which normally is used during visual flying.

In effect, the natural horizon is replaced by the attitude indicator, and the remaining instruments play the same role as during visual flight. The general information provided by the attitude indicator is correlated with the specific information gained from the altimeter, heading indicator, turn coordinator, and airspeed indicator. The correlated information is interpreted by the pilot to determine the relationship between the airplane's attitude and its performance. In order to control the attitude, the pilot must become skillful at reading the six flight instruments shown in figure 7-1, interpreting the indications, and applying this information to control of the airplane.

The table following figure 7-1, illustrates that the attitude indicator is the *control* instrument for maintaining airplane attitude, while the instruments used to determine the pitch and bank quality changes for various flight maneuvers. The table also illustrates that the majority of the pilot's scan is directed to the control instrument and the pitch and bank quality instruments.

CROSS-CHECK

Cross-checking, or scanning, is the term applied to the continuous systematic observation of flight instruments. The actual technique may vary somewhat with different individuals, various maneuvers, variations in airplane equipment, and the experience and proficiency level of the pilot.

At first, a pilot may have a tendency to cross-check rapidly, looking directly at the instrument without knowing exactly

Fig. 7-1. Flight Instruments

MANEUVER	CONTROL INSTRUMENT	PITCH QUALITY INSTRUMENT	BANK QUALITY INSTRUMENT	POWER QUALITY INSTRUMENT	ADDITIONAL QUALITY PITCH & BANK INSTRUMENTS
STRAIGHT-AND-LEVEL FLIGHT	ATTITUDE INDICATOR	ALTIMETER VERTICAL VELOCITY	HEADING INDICATOR	AIRSPEED INDICATOR	TURN COORDINATOR COORDINATED BALL
CLIMBS AND DESCENTS — CONSTANT AIRSPEED	ATTITUDE INDICATOR	AIRSPEED INDICATOR	HEADING INDICATOR	VERTICAL VELOCITY INDICATOR	TURN COORDINATOR ALTIMETER COORDINATED BALL
CLIMBS AND DESCENTS — CONSTANT RATE	ATTITUDE INDICATOR	VERTICAL VELOCITY INDICATOR	HEADING INDICATOR	AIRSPEED INDICATOR	TURN COORDINATOR HEADING INDICATOR
TURNS— CONSTANT ANGLE OF BANK	ATTITUDE INDICATOR COORDINATED BALL	ALTIMETER VERTICAL VELOCITY INDICATOR	ATTITUDE INDICATOR	AIRSPEED INDICATOR	HEADING INDICATOR TURN COORDINATOR
TURNS— CONSTANT RATE	ATTITUDE INDICATOR COORDINATED BALL	ALTIMETER VERTICAL VELOCITY INDICATOR	TURN COORDINATOR	AIRSPEED INDICATOR	HEADING INDICATOR
CLIMBING OR DESCENDING TURNS— CONSTANT AIRSPEED	ATTITUDE INDICATOR COORDINATED BALL	AIRSPEED INDICATOR	ATTITUDE INDICATOR	VERTICAL VELOCITY INDICATOR	HEADING INDICATOR ALTIMETER
CLIMBING OR DESCENDING TURNS— CONSTANT RATE	ATTITUDE INDICATOR COORDINATED BALL	VERTICAL VELOCITY INDICATOR	TURN COORDINATOR	AIRSPEED INDICATOR	HEADING INDICATOR ALTIMETER

|◄——————— MAJOR SCAN ———————►|◄—————— MINOR SCAN ——————►|

INSTRUMENT SCAN

what information he is seeking. However, with familiarity and practice, the instrument scan assumes definite trends during specific flight conditions and these trends are modified as the airplane makes a transition from one flight condition to another. The pilot also learns that during some phases of flight, the instrument scan must be more rapid than at other times.

Throughout their lifetimes, most individuals have learned to apply full concentration to a single task in order to perform it well. However, this tendency introduces a number of errors that can

be eliminated through awareness and conscious avoidance of the tendencies.

FIXATION

Fixation results from a natural human inclination to observe a specific instrument accurately. Fixation on a single instrument usually results in poor control. For example, while performing a medium bank or shallow bank turn, the pilot may have a tendency to watch the turn coordinator throughout the turn, instead of including other instruments in his cross-check. This fixation on the turn coordinator often leads to a loss of altitude through poor pitch and bank control.

EMPHASIS

Instead of relying on a combination of instruments necessary for airplane performance information, the pilot sometimes places too much emphasis on a single instrument. This differs from fixation in that the pilot is using other instruments for information, but is devoting too much attention to a particular instrument.

OMISSION

During performance of a maneuver, the pilot sometimes fails to anticipate significant instrument indications following marked attitude changes. For example, during leveloff from a climb or descent, emphasis may be placed on pitch control instruments, while omitting the instruments which supply heading or roll information. Such omissions result in erratic control of heading and bank.

In spite of these common errors, most pilots can adapt well to flight by instrument reference after instruction and practice. In fact, many beginning pilots find that they can control the airplane more easily and precisely by instruments. Occasionally, during visual flight, beginning pilots rely too heavily on instrument references when they should rely more on outside visual references and be vigilant for other air traffic.

INSTRUMENT INTERPRETATION

The pilot should understand each instrument's operating principles, and this knowledge must be coupled with awareness of what the particular instrument reveals about the airplane's performance. Each flight maneuver involves the use of combinations of instruments that must be read and interpreted in order to control the airplane's attitude. For example, if pitch attitude is to be determined, the attitude indicator, airspeed indicator, altimeter, and vertical velocity indicator provide the required information. These instruments are enclosed in the shaded area shown in figure 7-2.

Fig. 7-2. Pitch Instruments

Fig. 7-3. Bank Instruments

If bank attitude is to be determined, the attitude indicator, turn coordinator, and heading indicator must be interpreted, as shown in figure 7-3. It can be seen that to determine both pitch and bank attitude by instrument reference, all of the flight instruments must be included in the scan.

AIRPLANE CONTROL

To control an airplane by reference to instruments, the pilot must continue perfecting the techniques of proper pitch, bank, and power control as practiced during flight by visual reference. He should maintain a light touch on the controls and trim off any control pressures once the airplane has stabilized in a particular attitude. Abrupt and erratic airplane control and pilot fatigue can result if light control pressures are not utilized and control pressures are not relieved with trim.

SENSORY PERCEPTIONS

A human being's ability to maintain equilibrium depends primarily on three senses—the sense of sight, the sense of changing position which originates in the balance organs of the inner ear, and the postural sense (kinesthesia) which includes sensations of touch, pressure, and tension on muscles, joints, and tendons. When flying in VFR conditions, the pilot's orientation is maintained by utilizing these senses. The primary sense is sight, which uses the natural horizon of the earth as a reference. However, during instrument flight, the pilot must use the indications of his flight instruments to maintain his orientation with the earth.

During instrument flight, some of the sensations from the inner ear and postural sense tend to send conflicting information to the brain. Confusion results when the brain is unable to interpret whether the pressure and tension of the muscles is a result of gravity or of load factors induced during maneuvering. Therefore, the pilot must learn to trust his instruments and react accordingly.

STRAIGHT-AND-LEVEL FLIGHT

To accurately maintain straight-and-level flight by instrument reference, the pilot must learn to control the pitch, bank, and yaw of the airplane through interpretation of the flight instruments. The following discussion of airplane control and the flight instruments outlines the proper use and interpretation of the instrument indications as they relate to pitch and bank control.

PITCH CONTROL

At a constant airspeed and power setting, there is only one specific pitch attitude which will maintain level flight. The instruments used to maintain pitch control are the attitude indicator, airspeed indicator, altimeter, and vertical velocity indicator. Any change in the pitching motion of the airplane registers a change on these instruments in direct proportion to the magnitude of the change.

In a climb, the nose of the miniature airplane rises above the artificial horizon bar of the attitude indicator, as illustrated in figure 7-4. This causes a decrease in airspeed, an increase in altitude, and a positive rate-of-climb indication.

Conversely, a pitch change to a nose-down attitude causes the miniature airplane on the attitude indicator to move below the horizon bar. In addition, an increase in airspeed, a decrease in altitude, and an indication of a descent on the vertical velocity indicator are displayed on the flight instruments, as shown in figure 7-5.

ATTITUDE INDICATOR

The attitude indicator is the only instrument which provides a pictorial display of the airplane's overall attitude. All of the other instruments are used indirectly in determining attitude.

The relationship between the natural horizon and the artificial horizon bar during pitch changes often is demonstrated by the instructor during attitude instrument flight instruction. From this demonstration, the student will observe that the displacement of the horizon bar on the attitude indicator appears to be much smaller than displacement of the airplane's nose in relation to the natural horizon. Therefore, light control pressures should be used and the required attitude changes made slowly and smoothly.

Fig. 7-4. Climb Indications

Fig. 7-5. Descent Indications

When practicing pitch control using the attitude indicator, the pilot should initially restrict the displacement of the horizon bar to a one-half bar width up or down, progressing later to a full bar width. Greater displacement should be used only when significant attitude changes are required.

The control pressures necessary to make pitch changes vary in different airplanes. However, the pilot cannot feel control pressure changes if he has a tight grip on the control wheel. If light pressures are maintained and the airplane is retrimmed after it is stabilized in a new attitude, a smooth and precise attitude control technique results.

ALTIMETER

At a constant airspeed and power setting, any deviation from level flight will be the result of a pitch change. The altimeter provides an indirect indication of the quality of pitch attitude. Since the altitude should remain constant when the airplane is in level flight, a deviation from the desired altitude indicates the need for a pitch change.

Obviously, if the altitude is increasing, the nose must be lowered. The rate of movement of the altimeter needle is as important as its direction of movement in maintaining level flight. Large pitch attitude deviations from level flight result in rapid altitude changes; slight pitch deviations produce much slower changes in the altimeter needle movement.

ALTITUDE CORRECTION RULES

A common rule for altitude corrections of less than 100 feet is to use a one-half bar width adjustment on the attitude indicator; for corrections in excess of 100 feet, a full bar width correction should be used. As these corrections are established, the rate of altitude change on the vertical speed indicator and the altimeter may be observed in the instrument scan.

If the deviation from the desired altitude is less than 100 feet, the attitude adjustment needed to return to the correct altitude may be made without changing the power setting. However, if the deviation from the desired altitude is greater than 100 feet, a change in power setting and an appropriate pitch change should be made.

VERTICAL VELOCITY INDICATOR

The normal function of the vertical velocity indicator is to aid in establishing and maintaining a desired rate of climb or descent. Due to the design of the instrument, there is a lag of approximately six to nine seconds before the correct rate of change is registered. Even though this lag exists, the vertical velocity indicator may be used as a trend instrument for maintaining a desired pitch attitude. As a trend instrument, it indicates the direction of pitch change almost instantaneously, as illustrated in figure 7-6.

If the needle deviates from the zero position, the instrument is indicating that a pitch change is in progress. As the pilot applies corrective pressures while referring to the attitude indicator, this pressure will stop the needle movement and place the airplane in a level attitude again. However, the student is cautioned not to try to return the needle to zero, since the lag in the vertical velocity

Fig. 7-6. Vertical Velocity Indicator

indicator will induce a tendency to overcontrol. Instead, after a pitch correction has been made to return to level flight, an additional slight pitch correction should be made to return to the desired altitude. Pilot judgment and experience in a particular airplane dictate the rate of altitude correction. As a guide, the miniature airplane on the attitude indicator should be adjusted to produce a rate of change which is double the amount of altitude deviation, and power should be used as necessary. For example, if an airplane is descending at 300 f.p.m. and is 100 feet below the desired altitude, a climb rate of 200 f.p.m. should be selected. The initial amount of pitch change required to stop the descent and climb at 200 f.p.m. is estimated and held constant until the vertical velocity indicator displays an accurate rate, then adjusted as necessary.

AIRSPEED INDICATOR

When properly interpreted, the airspeed indicator represents another indirect indication of the quality of pitch attitude. If a constant power setting and pitch attitude are established and the airplane is permitted to stabilize, the airspeed remains constant. As the pitch attitude is raised, the airspeed decreases slightly. On the other hand, as the pitch attitude lowers, the airspeed increases somewhat.

A rapid change in airspeed is an indication that a large pitch change has occurred and that smooth control pressure in the opposite direction should be applied. Again, however, the amount of pitch change caused by the control pressure should be noted on the attitude indicator to avoid overcontrolling the airplane. If the airspeed indicator needle is moving in one direction, the instant that its movement stops, the airplane is passing through level flight. Therefore, when the airspeed indicator is included in the scan with the attitude indicator, altimeter, and vertical velocity indicator, it furnishes positive pitch control information to the pilot.

BANK CONTROL INSTRUMENTS

It is a fundamental fact of airplane control that banking the wings will create a turning moment. Therefore, in order to fly a given heading, the pilot should attempt to keep the wings of the airplane level with the horizon while maintaining coordinated flight.

ATTITUDE INDICATOR

The principal instrument used for bank control is the attitude indicator. It is supported in this function by the heading indicator and turn coordinator. On most attitude indicators, the angle of bank is shown by the alignment of the bank index with the bank scale at the top of the instrument and by the relationship of the wings of the miniature airplane to the horizon bar, as illustrated in figure 7-7.

Fig. 7-7. Attitude Indicator

HEADING INDICATOR

The quality of bank attitude of an airplane in coordinated flight also is indirectly indicated on the heading indicator. Generally, if the heading displayed on the heading indicator is not changing, the wings are level. On the other hand, a slow heading change indicates a shallow bank angle, while a rapid change in heading indicates a steep bank.

TURN COORDINATOR

When the miniature airplane in the turn coordinator is in a wings-level position, the airplane is maintaining a constant heading. If the wings of the miniature airplane are displaced from the level flight position, the airplane is turning in the direction that the miniature airplane is banking.

The turn coordinator also indicates the rate of turn. When a wingtip of the miniature airplane is aligned with one of the white marks at the side of the instrument below the level attitude mark, the airplane is turning at the standard rate of three degrees per second. A standard-rate turn indication is illustrated in figure 7-8.

The principal reference for making bank corrections is the attitude indicator. To make a heading change, a bank angle equal to one-half of the difference between the present heading and the desired heading is used. However, this angle should not exceed that necessary for a standard-rate turn. For example, if the desired airplane heading is 300° and the present heading is 290°, the required heading change is 10°. Therefore, the bank angle used to return to the desired heading should be no greater than one-half of 10° or, in this example, 5° of bank.

INCLINOMETER

The ball of the turn coordinator is actually a separate instrument called an inclinometer. However, the inclinometer and the miniature airplane are used together. It should be recalled that the ball indicates whether coordinated flight is being maintained. If the ball is off center, as shown in figure 7-9, the airplane is slipping and correction should be made with appropriate coordinated rudder and aileron pressure.

Fig. 7-9. Slip Indication

CLIMBS

To enter a climb from cruising airspeed, the nose is raised to a two-bar width, nose-high pitch attitude, as indicated in figure 7-10. This adjustment is a general guideline and varies with the airplane used, the desired rate of climb, and the desired climb airspeed.

Light control pressures are used to initiate and maintain the climb, since pressures change as the airplane decelerates. Power may be advanced to the climb

Fig. 7-8. Standard-Rate Turn

Fig. 7-10. Initial Climb Attitude

power setting simultaneously with the pitch change, provided maximum r.p.m. is not exceeded. Power also can be added after the pitch change is established and the airspeed approaches the climb speed.

If the transition has been made smoothly, the vertical velocity indicator will show an immediate upward trend and will stabilize at a rate appropriate to the stabilized airspeed and pitch attitude. As the transition is made from cruise to climb, additional right rudder pressure is added in order to maintain the desired heading.

Directional control is maintained during a climb entry by reference to the attitude indicator, heading indicator, and turn coordinator. Once the climb has

Fig. 7-11. Stabilized Straight Climb

been established and stabilized, control pressures are trimmed away.

The typical instrument indications of a training airplane in a stabilized straight climb are shown in figure 7-11. If the instrument scan reveals any deviation from the desired heading or pitch attitude, the required correction is made by reference to the attitude indicator while continuing the scan.

LEVELOFF FROM CLIMBS

To level off from a climb at a designated altitude, the student should initiate the leveloff before reaching the desired altitude. The airplane will continue to climb at a decreasing rate throughout the transition to level flight. An effective guideline is to lead the altitude by 10 percent of the vertical velocity indication. For example, if the airplane is climbing at 500 feet per minute, the student should begin the leveloff 50 feet prior to reaching the desired altitude. To level off and accelerate to cruise speed, smooth, steady forward elevator pressure is applied. During the transition from climb to cruise, right rudder pressure is relaxed and the heading indicator is checked to assure the desired heading is maintained. As level flight is established using the attitude indicator, the airspeed increases to cruise speed and the vertical velocity needle moves slowly toward zero. At this time, rough trim adjustments may be made. Then, as cruise speed is reached, power is reduced to the recommended cruise setting and final trim adjustments are made.

DESCENTS

To enter a descent, the pilot adjusts the airspeed to a predetermined descent airspeed using pitch and power adjustments. The descent attitude is established using the attitude indicator, and the power setting is adjusted to a value that results in the approximate desired speed. As the pitch attitude and descent rate stabilize, the airplane is trimmed.

During a *constant airspeed* descent, any deviation from the desired airspeed requires a pitch adjustment. For a *constant rate* descent at a specified airspeed, the vertical velocity indicator becomes the principal instrument for pitch control as it stabilizes at the desired rate. Airspeed adjustments are made primarily with changes in pitch attitude, and the rate of descent corrections are made by changing the power setting. Figure 7-12 illustrates the instrument indications representative of a stabilized descent in a typical light training airplane.

Fig. 7-12. Stabilized Straight Descent

LEVELOFF FROM DESCENTS

As in other leveloff procedures, the pilot begins leveling off from a descent prior to reaching the desired altitude; the amount of lead depends on the rate of descent. In a standard 500 f.p.m. rate of descent, the leveloff normally is lead by 50 to 100 feet. As the leadpoint is reached, power is added to the appropriate level flight cruise setting. Since the nose tends to pitch up as the airspeed increases, very little back elevator pressure is required until approximately 50 feet above the desired altitude. At this point, the pitch attitude is adjusted smoothly to a level flight attitude for the airspeed selected.

The attitude indicator is included frequently in the scan as the leveloff procedure is accomplished. After the pitch attitude and airspeed have stabilized in straight-and-level flight, control pressures are removed by trimming.

TURNS

To enter a turn, the pilot should apply coordinated aileron and rudder pressure in the desired direction of turn. The attitude indicator is used to establish the approximate angle of bank required for a standard-rate turn. This angle of bank is achieved by aligning the appropriate bank angle mark with the index at the top of the attitude indicator, as shown in figure 7-13.

Additional lift is required to offset the loss of vertical lift component in the turn, so the pitch attitude is raised slightly to maintain altitude. As the turn is established, it is necessary to adjust the nose of the miniature airplane so it is slightly above the level flight position on the horizon bar. As the turn is progressing, the turn coordinator is checked to determine if a standard rate is being maintained and, if not, a bank adjustment is made on the attitude indicator.

The pilot also includes the heading indicator in his scan to determine progress toward the desired heading. Furthermore, the altimeter is checked to determine that the adjusted pitch attitude has compensated properly for the loss of vertical lift component and that a constant altitude is being maintained throughout the turn.

The principal instrument reference for the roll-out is the attitude indicator. Since a slightly nose-high attitude has been held throughout the turn, elevator

Fig. 7-13. Level Standard-Rate Turn

back pressure is relaxed to prevent an altitude gain as the airplane is returned to straight-and-level flight. As the wings-level position is attained, the pilot continues his instrument scan. When the airplane stabilizes in the cruise flight configuration, any control pressures required to maintain straight-and-level flight flight are trimmed away.

A guideline for determining the amount of lead required for roll-out from a turn is to use approximately one-half the angle of bank. For example, if a standard-rate turn is being made at a bank angle of 15°, the pilot should begin the roll-out approximately eight degrees before reaching the desired heading, as shown in figure 7-14.

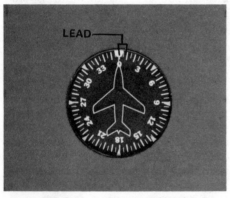

Fig. 7-14. Leading the Roll-Out

CLIMBING AND DESCENDING TURNS

The proper execution of climbing and descending turns combines the techniques used in straight climbs and descents with turning techniques. Initially, the climb or descent is established and, as pitch attitude is stabilized, the pilot rolls into the turn. However, proficiency should be developed so that the climb or descent can be established simultaneously with the turn. The pilot must carefully consider aerodynamic factors that affect lift and power control. The rate of cross-check and interpretation also must be increased to enable him to control both pitch and bank changes.

CRITICAL ATTITUDES AND RECOVERIES

Any airplane attitude not normally used is considered a critical attitude. Such an attitude may result from any number of conditions, such as turbulence, disorientation, confusion, preoccupation with cabin duties, carelessness in cross-check, errors in instrument interpretation, or lack of proficiency in basic airplane control. By the time the pilot realizes the need to concentrate on the instruments, the attitude of his airplane may be such that immediate attention and recovery are required.

During the more advanced phases of private pilot training, the student may be instructed to take his hands and feet off the controls and close his eyes while the instructor puts the airplane in a critical attitude. The instructor may require the student to move his head up and down to induce disorientation.

As soon as control of the airplane is returned to the pilot, he should check the airspeed and attitude indicators to determine pitch and bank. Then, he should make immediate corrections to return the airplane to straight-and-level flight.

The types of critical attitude recoveries most commonly practiced are approaches to climbing stalls and well-developed power-on spirals. The pilot will be required to demonstrate recovery from these attitudes during the FAA flight test.

NOSE-HIGH CRITICAL ATTITUDE

An unusually high pitch attitude displayed on the attitude indicator is evidence of a nose-high critical attitude. Before initiating a correction, however, the pilot should check the other instruments to confirm the reliability of the attitude indicator. The instrument indications of a typical nose-high critical attitude are shown in figure 7-15. The primary objective for recovery from this

Fig. 7-15. Nose-High Critical Attitude

Fig. 7-16. Nose-Low Critical Attitude

attitude is to prevent a stall. Therefore, the pilot should simultaneously decrease pitch to reduce angle of attack, increase power, and roll the wings level.

NOSE-LOW CRITICAL ATTITUDE

The indications of a nose-low critical attitude, as shown in figure 7-16, are a nose-low pitch attitude, increasing airspeed, rapid loss of altitude, and a high rate of descent. The primary objective in nose-low critical attitude recovery is to avoid an excessively high airspeed or load factor. In this case, the pilot should simultaneously reduce power, roll wings level, increase pitch attitude to stop acceleration, and gently raise the nose to the level flight attitude. If the pilot raises the nose before rolling the wings level, the increased load factor can result in an accelerated stall, a spin, or a force exceeding the airplane design load factor.

A well-developed power-on spiral resulting from a nose-low critical attitude often is encountered by a noninstrument rated pilot who continues flight into adverse weather conditions. In this situation, the pilot senses the increased speed of the airplane due to the increased slipstream noise and obviously high engine r.p.m. The normal reaction to a nose-down attitude is to apply elevator back pressure. However, in this instance back pressure will result only in a continually tightening spiral.

ACCEPTABLE PERFORMANCE FOR INSTRUMENT FLIGHT

The pilot's performance is evaluated on the basis of coordination, smoothness, and accuracy. He should perform turns of at least 180° to within 20° of a preselected heading, and climbs and descents to within 100 feet of a preselected altitude.

chapter 8

INTRODUCTION

In many respects, night flight is easier and more pleasant than daytime flying. Traffic is usually easier to locate at night and the air is generally smoother and cooler, resulting in more comfortable flight and better airplane performance. Furthermore, the night pilot experiences less airport traffic pattern congestion and often finds less competition when using communication frequencies.

The aesthetic advantages of night flight also appeal to many pilots. This is especially true on a smooth, clear night when the pilot can turn the cabin lights down, relax, and enjoy the satisfactions of flying in the night environment.

Just a few years ago, most general aviation pilots considered night flying an emergency procedure. Since then, great strides have been made in navigation, lighting, marking, and radio communication. These developments have made night flying in light airplanes a routine operation. In addition, airports, obstructions, and airplanes are now equipped with standard lighting.

NIGHT FLIGHT CONSIDERATIONS

On a bright, moonlit evening when the visibility is good and the wind is calm, night flying is not a great deal different than flying during the day. However, the inexperienced pilot must consider the following factors carefully before making a night flight.

1. Visibility
2. Amount of outside light available
3. Surface winds
4. General weather situation
5. Availability of lighted airports enroute
6. Proper functioning of the airplane and its systems
7. Night flying equipment in the airplane
8. The pilot's recent night flying experience

PREFLIGHT INSPECTION

The preflight inspection should be performed in the usual manner, preferably in a well-lighted area with the aid of a flashlight. The pilot should insure a spare set of fuses is aboard the airplane. If the airplane is equipped with circuit breakers, they should be checked to see that they are not tripped. A tripped circuit breaker usually is an indication of an equipment malfunction, since most circuit breakers cannot be tripped manually. When a tripped circuit breaker is discovered during the preflight, it should be reset and the associated equipment tested for proper operation prior to flight.

The windshield should be checked for dirt that may interfere with vision. Although this is a good preflight procedure anytime, it is especially important before a night flight.

POSITION LIGHTS

All aircraft operating between sunset and sunrise are required to have operable navigation lights, or position lights. These lights should be turned on prior to the preflight inspection so they can be checked visually to insure proper operation. Many pilots prefer to check the position lights immediately, then turn them off to avoid excessive drain on the battery.

Position lights should be on anytime the engine is operating or the airplane is moving. A red position light is located on the left wingtip, a *white* light on the

tail, and a *green* light on the right wingtip, as shown in figure 8-1. Many airplanes incorporate position light detectors, which are plastic attachments for the navigation lights to convey light above or below the surface of the wing. These attachments allow the pilot to check for proper operation of the lights from inside the airplane.

LANDING AND TAXI LIGHTS

Most airplanes have landing lights and some have taxi lights to illuminate the runway and taxiway. These lights may be mounted behind a common lens in the leading edge of the wing, or in the cowling. Another installation which usually is restricted to high performance airplanes is described as a retractable gear mounted light. All three types of lights are depicted in figure 8-2.

Although both the landing light and the taxi light must be checked visually for correct operation during the preflight inspection, these lights should not be allowed to operate for any length of time with the engine shut down because of the high electrical energy drain on the battery. The preflight check should include inspection for illumination, cracks in the lens, and the correct aiming angle of each light. However, care should be taken during the operation of landing and taxi lights to avoid shining them in the direction of another aircraft, since this can impair the other pilot's night vision.

ANTICOLLISION LIGHTING

All aircraft must have anticollision lights for night operation. The most common type is a rotating beacon which normally emits red flashes of light at a rate of approximately one flash per second.

An increasing number of airplanes, however, are being equipped with brilliant, flashing, white strobe lights which can be

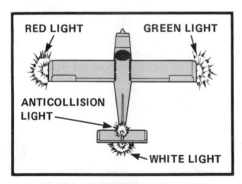

Fig. 8-1. Airplane Navigation Lights

Fig. 8-2. Landing Lights and Taxi Lights

seen for many miles at night. These lights also can be used in poor visibility conditions during the day. Lighting systems should be checked during the preflight inspection.

INSTRUMENT PANEL LIGHTS

All modern airplanes are equipped with some system for lighting the instrument panel and instruments. Prior to any night flight, the panel lighting system should be checked to determine that it is operating satisfactorily. A flashlight should be carried on night flights to provide an alternate source of light if interior lights malfunction. Some pilots prefer to place a layer of red cellophane between the flashlight bulb and its lens because red light is less detrimental to night vision than white light.

Panel lighting generally is controlled by a rheostat switch which allows the pilot to select the intensity of light which best satisfies his needs. These may be separate rheostats for the flight instruments, engine instruments, and radios.

The light intensity should be adjusted just bright enough so the pilot is able to read the instrument indications. If the lighting is too bright, a glare results and night vision suffers. One of three types of panel lighting normally is used.

FLOOD LIGHTING

Flood lighting is a common method of illuminating the entire instrument panel with one light source. In this system, a single ceiling-mounted light is used with a rheostat to regulate its intensity. Its beam is directed over both the flight and engine instruments. Flood lighting seems to produce the most glare if the intensity is too high.

POST LIGHTING

Post lighting is installed in slightly higher performance aircraft. Each instrument has its individual light source, which is adjacent to the instrument. Each post light beam is directed at the instrument and is shaded from the pilot's eyes.

Generally, there are two rheostats for this lighting system—one for the flight instruments and another for the engine instruments. In addition, there may be separate controls for illumination of fuel tank selectors, switch panels, radios, and convenience lighting.

INTERNAL LIGHTING

Internal instrument lighting is similar to post lighting, except that the light source is located *inside* the instrument itself. Again, the intensity of light usually is controlled in two groups—flight and engine instruments.

The magnetic compass and radios generally utilize internal lighting. Luminescent lettering is often used with internal lighting to permit instrument interpretation with less light. This type of lighting normally produces the least amount of glare and is found in many currently manufactured airplanes.

NIGHT VISION

The ability to see at night can be greatly improved if the pilot understands and applies certain techniques. For example, if the pilot's eyes are exposed to strong light, even briefly, night vision is temporarily destroyed. For this reason, avoidance of strong light must begin well in advance of a night flight.

It has been found that the dark adaptation required for night vision is destroyed most quickly and completely by exposure to white light, while dark red light has been found to be the least detrimental. Although red light is most desirable for preservation of dark adaptation, its use results in disturbance of normal color relationships. Therefore, carefully designed systems of white or blue-white light are finding wider application for cabin illumination.

OFF-CENTER VISION

Central vision normally is used to see objects. However, central vision is ineffective under low illumination. For this reason, the pilot should not look directly at objects at night. The objects can be seen more clearly if the gaze is directed slightly above, below, or to one side of the object. It has been found that looking about 10° off center permits better viewing in low levels of lighting.

This effect can be demonstrated by counting a cluster of very faint lights in the distance at night. When looking slightly off center, more lights are seen clearly than when looking directly at the cluster.

CABIN FAMILIARIZATION

Following the preflight inspection, one of the first steps in preparation for night flight is becoming *thoroughly familiar* with the airplane's cabin, instrumentation, and control layout. It is recommended that the pilot practice locating each instrument, control, and switch both with and without cabin lights. Since the markings on some switches and circuit breaker panels may be hard to read at night, the pilot should assure himself that he is able to locate and use these devices and read the markings in poor lighting conditions.

AIRPORT LIGHTING

ROTATING BEACONS

Most airports are equipped with rotating beacons to make them easier to locate at night. Civil airports for land airplanes

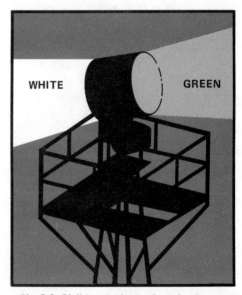

Fig. 8-3. Civil Land Airport Rotating Beacon

WHITE   GREEN

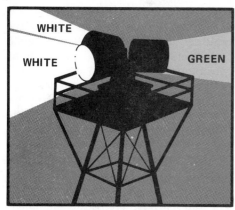

Fig. 8-4. Military Land Airport
Rotating Beacon

produce alternating green and white flashes, as shown in figure 8-3. Military airports can be distinguished from civil airports because their beacons emit two white flashes alternating with a single green flash, as shown in figure 8-4.

TAXIWAYS AND RUNWAYS

The painted markings on runways, ramps, and taxiways are not especially useful to pilots at night, since they are difficult to see. Therefore, various types of lighting aids are used to mark and identify different segments of the airport for night operations, as shown in figure 8-5.

Taxiways are marked along their edges with blue lights to distinguish them from runways, which have white lights along the edges. The intensity of taxiway and runway lights usually can be controlled by the tower and may be adjusted upon request of the pilot. The threshold of a runway is marked with two or more green lights, and obstructions or unusable areas are marked with red lights.

OTHER LIGHTING AIDS

Wind indicators, such as wind socks, wind tees, and tetrahedrons, often are lighted so that they are clearly visible from the surface and from traffic pattern altitude. (See Fig. 8-6.) However, radio voice communication, when available, should be considered an effective supple-

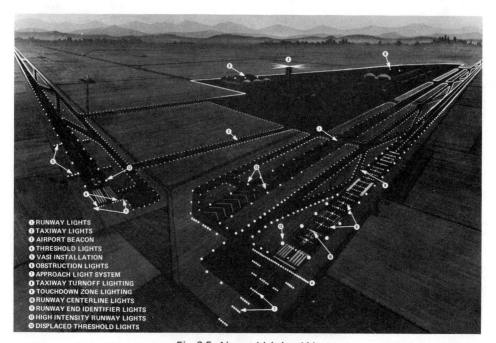

1. RUNWAY LIGHTS
2. TAXIWAY LIGHTS
3. AIRPORT BEACON
4. THRESHOLD LIGHTS
5. VASI INSTALLATION
6. OBSTRUCTION LIGHTS
7. APPROACH LIGHT SYSTEM
8. TAXIWAY TURNOFF LIGHTING
9. TOUCHDOWN ZONE LIGHTING
10. RUNWAY CENTERLINE LIGHTS
11. RUNWAY END IDENTIFIER LIGHTS
12. HIGH INTENSITY RUNWAY LIGHTS
13. DISPLACED THRESHOLD LIGHTS

Fig. 8-5. Airport Lighting Aids

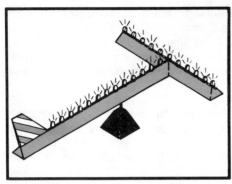

Fig. 8-6. Wind Tee With Lights

ment for obtaining surface wind and active runway information at night.

NIGHT OPERATIONS

ENGINE STARTUP

Caution should be used in the engine startup procedure at night, since it is difficult for other persons to determine that the pilot intends to start the engine. In addition to the usual *"clear prop,"* turning on the position lights or momentarily turning on the landing light can help warn others that the propeller is about to rotate. An alternate procedure, which conserves electrical energy, is to shine the flashlight through the windshield and around the area of the propeller prior to starting the engine.

TAXI TECHNIQUE

After the engine is started and the oil pressure is checked, other necessary electrical equipment should be turned on. However, the taxi light normally should be left off until the pilot is actually ready to taxi.

Airplane taxi and landing lights normally cast a beam that is narrow and concentrated. Because of this fact, taxi light illumination to the side is minimal and taxi speed should be slower at night, especially in congested ramp and parking areas. Initially, judgment of distances is more difficult and it takes some adaptation to taxi within the limitations of the area covered by the taxi light.

When operating at an unfamiliar airport at night, it is wise to ask for instructions or advice about taxi procedures to avoid taxiing onto unpaved surfaces, areas of construction, or unlighted and unmarked portions of the ramp and taxiway. Ground controllers or UNICOM operators usually are cooperative in furnishing pilots with this type of information.

PRETAKEOFF CHECK

When the airplane is stopped at the runup area, the taxi or landing lights and any unnecessary electrical equipment should be turned off to conserve electrical power until the runup is completed. In addition to the usual checklist procedures, the radios should be checked carefully for operation. During the run-up, the pilot should watch for a drop in the intensity of the lighting equipment when power is reduced to idle. A pronounced drop in intensity may indicate that the battery needs charging.

TAKEOFF

The differences between day and night flight can be minimized by scheduling a night checkout which begins at twilight. When this procedure is utilized, the takeoffs, landings, and traffic pattern work begin in the more familiar daylight environment and, as darkness increases, the transition to the conditions associated with night operation is made gradually. This procedure is highly recommended.

As the takeoff roll is initiated, the pilot should select a reference point down the runway, such as the point where the runway edge lights seem to converge. If he looks directly toward the lights near the airplane, he will experience an illusion of great speed. However, these lights can be used to keep the airplane properly aligned during the takeoff roll.

During his first night takeoff, the pilot may notice the lack of reliable outside visual references after he is airborne. This is particularly true at small airports located in sparsely populated areas. To compensate for this effect, he should use the flight instruments in conjunction with available outside visual references after takeoff.

Immediately after liftoff, the usual ground references disappear. The pilot should maintain a normal climb attitude on the attitude indicator. The vertical speed indicator and altimeter should indicate a climb and the airspeed indicator should also be included in the cross-check. The first 500 feet of altitude after takeoff is considered to be the critical period in transitioning from the comparatively well-lighted airport area into what sometimes appears as total darkness.

VISUAL IMPRESSIONS

During early training in night flight, most pilots find the initial visual impressions after traffic pattern departure to be strikingly different than those they are accustomed to during daytime flying. Therefore, orientation in the local flying area helps the pilot relate chart information to actual terrain and landmarks under night conditions.

The outlines of major cities and towns are clearly discernible and, during favorable weather, major metropolitan areas are visible from distances up to 100 miles or more, depending upon the flight altitude. Major highways tend to stand out at night because of the presence of numerous automobile headlights. Less traveled roads are usually not seen easily at night unless the moonlight is bright enough to reveal them.

On clear, moonlit nights, outlines of the terrain and other surface features are dimly visible. For example, a pilot often can discern the outlines of bodies of water by noting the reflection of the moonlight. However, on extremely dark nights, terrain features are nearly invisible, except in brightly lighted, populated areas.

COLLISION AVOIDANCE AT NIGHT

The position of other aircraft at night can be determined by scanning for position lights and anticollision lights. Since the arrangement of the red and green airplane position lights is the same as that used on boats and ships, the "Red right—returning" memory aid of sailing days is applicable. In other words, if the pilot observes red and green navigation lights and the red light is positioned on the right, the airplane is approaching, as illustrated by airplane 1 in figure 8-7. If the white position light is visible, the aircraft is on a heading that will take it away from the pilot's immediate area, as illustrated by airplane 2 in figure 8-7.

OVERFLIGHT OF THE AIRPORT

The general perspective of the airport at night and the location of runway edge lights, threshold lights, taxiway lights, ramps, and hangars can be determined by flying directly over the airport. This overflight should be made at least 500 feet above the existing traffic pattern altitude at uncontrolled airports and at more than 3,000 feet AGL at airports with operating control towers.

NIGHT MANEUVERS

In many ways, night flight is similar to flying in marginal VFR conditions. There are times when the discipline of an instrument rated pilot is needed because the senses may urge the pilot to believe his physical sensations, rather than the instrument indications.

Preparation for night flying should include a review of basic instrument flight techniques. This simulated instrument session should include straight-and-level flight, turns, climbs, climbing turns, descents, and descending turns. Many instructors require the student to make turns to specific headings while under

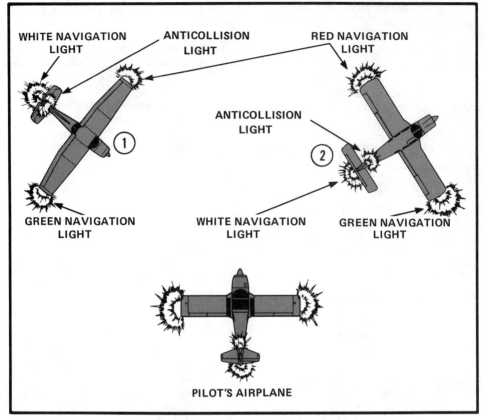

Fig. 8-7. Position Lights and Direction of Flight

the hood in order to teach the pilot to respond to possible radar assistance.

Critical attitude recovery helps the pilot cope with possible spatial disorientation. To enter a critical attitude, the instructor asks the student to take his hands and feet off the controls, close his eyes, and lower his head. Then, the instructor places the airplane in a critical attitude and allows the student to recover to straight-and-level flight unassisted by outside visual references. This procedure teaches the student to rely on instrument indications if spatial disorientation occurs.

WEATHER

The pilot operating at night must be especially attentive to signs of changing weather conditions. A pilot who is accus-tomed to daytime flight operations generally is not aware that it is extremely easy to fly into an overcast at night because the clouds cannot be detected easily by direct visual observation. There are several guidelines that will assist the night pilot if he inadvertently flies into heavy haze, patches of clouds, or an overcast.

A pilot approaching an overcast can sometimes detect the presence of the clouds because the lights in the distance disappear. In addition, a luminous glow, or halo, around the position lights indicates imminent or actual penetration of IFR weather conditions.

Another indirect visual cue can be obtained by turning on the landing light for a short period of time. On a very clear night, the beam of a landing light is barely scattered by particles in the air. However, if there is considerable haze or the temperature and dewpoint are converging rapidly and cloud formation is imminent, some scattering of the beam will be noticed. If actual penetration of a cloud layer occurs, the light beam will be dispersed in all directions. If inadvertent penetration of IFR conditions occurs, the pilot should calmly, but immediately, initiate a 180° standard-rate turn in order to fly out of the weather condition.

Before flying at night, the pilot should obtain a thorough weather briefing. He should give special attention to any indications in the weather briefing that indicate possible formation of clouds, overcast, fog, or precipitation.

ENROUTE PROCEDURES

In order to provide improved margins of safety, the choice of high cruising altitudes is recommended. There are several reasons for this recommendation. First, range is greater at higher altitudes. Second, gliding distance is greater, in the event of engine failure. Third, pilotage and radio navigation often are less difficult.

A major consideration in planning a night flight is to insure that an adequate supply of fuel is on board. A useful guideline is to reduce the daytime range of the airplane by one-third when flying at night. This procedure has two advantages. First, the pilot is not tempted to stretch his range; and second, the additional fuel can be useful in circumnavigating adverse weather.

The use of a subdued white cabin light for reading charts is recommended, since considerable information on charts is printed in red and disappears under red cabin lighting. If a map reading light is not available in the airplane, the pilot should use his flashlight for reading the charts. Special emphasis should be placed on the terrain elevations provided on the charts to insure adequate obstruction clearance.

EMERGENCY LANDINGS

If a forced landing is necessary at night, the same procedures as recommended for daytime emergency landings apply. If available, the landing light should be turned on during final approach to assist in avoiding obstacles in the final approach path.

Although highways look like tempting emergency landing strips at night, only the four-lane superhighway offers even reasonable assurance of the absence of powerlines across the highway. If a superhighway is selected, the landing should be made in the same direction as the flow of traffic.

Some pilots select a route for night flight that keeps them within reach of an airport as much of the time as possible. For example, a course comprised of a series of 25° zig-zags in the direction of various airports is only 10 percent longer than a straight course.

Higher cruising altitudes also are advantageous. At 10,000 feet, a light airplane with a glide ratio of 8 to 1 may glide as much as 16 miles. This distance may place the airplane within range of an airport.

NORMAL LANDINGS AT NIGHT

In some respects, night landings are actually easier than daytime landings, since the air is generally smooth and the disrupting effects of turbulence and excessive crosswinds usually are absent. However, there are a few special considerations and techniques that apply to landings at night.

Carefully controlled studies have revealed that pilots have a tendency to make lower approaches at night than during the daytime. Therefore, careful consideration should be given to traffic pattern procedures and to the factors that enable the pilot to maintain the proper glide angle on final approach.

Flying a standardized approach pattern is recommended, using the altimeter and vertical speed indicator to monitor the rate of descent. If the downwind leg is flown at 1,000 feet, a rectangular descent pattern beginning at the point opposite the touchdown point is recommended. When the intended touchdown point is in line with the wing, power can be reduced to establish a descent rate of approximately 500 feet per minute. When the touchdown point is about 45° behind the wing, the pilot should turn base at an altitude of approximately 600 feet AGL.

After the base leg is flown and the turn to final is complete, the altitude should be 300 to 400 feet AGL. The pattern should be flown at the same distance from the runway as during daylight to create a rectangular approach with a steady rate of descent. Maintenance of proper pitch attitude to stabilize the airspeed is as appropriate for night approaches as for those made during the day.

The runway lights provide an effective peripheral vision cue for gauging the approach and leveloff phases of the landing, as shown in figure 8-8. The runway lights, as seen with peripheral vision, seem to rise and spread laterally as the pilot nears the proper touchdown point.

Most pilots use the landing lights for night landing; however, there is an inherent disadvantage in use of this equipment. The portion of the runway illuminated by the landing lights seem higher than the dark area surrounding it. This effect tends to cause the pilot to flareout high. In addition, focusing attention on the area immediately in front of the airplane is poor practice, but the arrangement of most landing lights tends to encourage this technique. When using landing lights, the pilot's sighting point should be at least at the forward limit of the lighted area.

Fig. 8-8. Landing at Night

Fig. 8-9. Runway Lighting Illusions

Proper preparation for night flight should include landings made both with and without the aid of the landing lights. The cues for the proper maintenance of the approach profile are derived from the altimeter indications as previously discussed, and when on final, from the perspective created by the size, shape, and patterns of the runway lights. The altimeter and the vertical speed indicator should be checked against the position in the pattern to monitor the approach.

A no-light landing can be made in the manner described or modified slightly in the flareout and touchdown phases. A normal approach is held until over the threshold where the flareout normally begins. At this point, the airplane is slowed by using a slightly higher-than-normal pitch attitude. This attitude should remain constant until touchdown. With his hand on the throttle, the pilot adds power, as needed, and lowers the plane to the runway by maintaining a very shallow sink rate. He should be careful to avoid an increasing sink rate or the approach of a stall.

Proficiency in performing landings without landing lights requires practice. After the first few approaches and touchdowns, they can be executed accurately. Familiarity with the technique allows the pilot to make a safe night landing with the landing lights inoperative.

ILLUSIONS

There are several illusions connected with night approaches and landings. For example, the runway lights appear to form a flat plane that can be mistaken for the runway itself, as shown in figure 8-9. However, the runway is actually lower than the plane created by these lights because the lights usually are mounted on short poles slightly above the actual runway surface.

Another common illusion is the feeling of moving faster along the runway than the actual speed. This illusion occurs because only nearby objects, such as boundary lights or centerline lights, can be seen clearly and they seem to move past the airplane quite rapidly.

In addition, a normal approach looks steeper at night and creates an illusion of overshooting, which may actually result in undershooting and landing short of the runway. This illusion is thought to be responsible for the general tendency of pilots to make lower approaches at night, even though they believe they are on the correct approach profile.

The lack of clearly defined ground reference points in the approach path may induce the pilot to maintain a higher-than-normal approach speed. The correct approach pitch attitude to control and stabilize the airspeed should be maintained as carefully at night as during the day.

Another illusion may be created by the slope of the runway. For example, a runway that slopes up and away from the threshold can make the pilot believe he is too high. On the other hand, a pilot approaching a downward sloping runway may think the approach is too low. The remedies for these illusions are careful attention to flying a normal traffic pattern and using aids such as VASI lights where they are available.

VASI LIGHTS

Both two- and three-bar VASI installations normally are set at three degrees, although angles at some locations may be as high as four and one-half degrees to provide proper obstacle clearance. The three-bar system provides two glide paths; pilots of smaller aircraft use the middle and near bars. Indications are the same as those of a standard two-bar installation. The far and middle bars provide a glide path which usually is one-quarter degree higher. This upper glide path is intended for use only by high cockpit aircraft.

The VASI system is especially valuable to a pilot operating at night, since most of the normal terrain profile cues used to determine the height of the airplane on final approach are subdued or invisible.

The standard two-bar VASI installation consists of four light bars or boxes, two placed on each side of the runway. The first set, or row, of VASI lights are the near bars and are placed about 600 feet beyond the threshold. The second row, referred to as the far bars, is located about 1,300 feet from the threshold, as illustrated in figure 8-10. The four groups of lights form a rectangle around the touchdown zone and provide a visual aiming point.

Each VASI box has a filter that effectively splits the light beams into a white

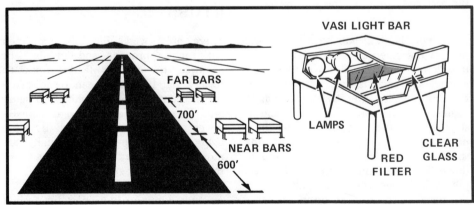

Fig. 8-10. Visual Approach Slope Indicator

Fig. 8-11. On Glide Path

segment above a certain angle and a red segment below this angle. If an aircraft on final approach overshoots a VASI box, the light beam appears *white* to the pilot. On the other hand, a low approach reveals the *red* segment of the light beam.

Since the objective is to land *between* the near and far bars, the far bars should appear red and the near bars should look white when viewed by the pilot on the proper final approach profile. *Red over white,* then, is the proper light combination observed when the airplane is on the glide path, as illustrated in figure 8-11.

If both rows appear white, as shown in figure 8-12, the airplane is too high and will overshoot the intended landing area. If both rows look red, the airplane is too low and the landing will be short, as shown in figure 8-13. When the approach path of the airplane is not stabilized and

the airplane is passing through the glide slope, the pilot can see the lights change color. For example, if the airplane is above the glide slope and all the lights appear white, the descent rate should be increased. As the airplane approaches the proper glide slope, the far bars transition from white to pink and then to red. After the airplane is on the proper glide slope, the far bars remain red and the near bars appear white. Conversely, if the airplane descends below the glide slope, the near bars transition from white through pink to red to provide an all-red indication.

If the airplane is at pattern altitude while still several miles from the threshold, all of the VASI lights appear red since the VASI glide slope angle at that point passes above the airplane. By flying toward the runway at a constant pattern altitude, the pilot can see the near bars gradually change from red to pink to white and he can transition from level flight to final approach descent as the glide slope is intercepted.

VASI lights should be used when available because they make a precise approach much easier to perform at night or when visibility is restricted. They also provide a visual descent profile that assures proper obstruction clearance in the approach area. VASI installations also provide visual reference for approaches made over water or other fea-

Fig. 8-12. Above Glide Path

Fig. 8-13. Below Glide Path

tureless terrain where adequate visual references are not available or can be misleading.

A special rule applies at airports with operating control towers and VASI-equipped runways. At these airports an airplane approaching to land on a runway served by a visual approach slope indicator, is required by regulations to maintain an altitude at or above the glide slope until a lower altitude is necessary for a safe landing.

ACCEPTABLE PERFORMANCE FOR NIGHT FLYING

The pilot should be able to demonstrate the preparation for a night local or cross-country flight. This requires that he be familiar with airport lighting, the airplane's lighting system and its operation, the need for a personal flashlight, and the weather conditions pertinent to night flight. Particular attention should be given to the temperature/dewpoint spread because of the possibility of ground fog formation.

The pilot must be able to explain the significance of the items peculiar to preparation for night flights. In addition, he should be able to demonstrate night VFR navigation, as required for cross-country flight operations. The pilot also should be able to explain and demonstrate the various techniques and aspects of night takeoffs and landings. He must understand the importance of constant vigilance for other aircraft on the ground and in the air, and the precautions necessary to avoid wake turbulence and spatial disorientation.

PART II – WORKBOOK

INTRODUCTION

These workbook exercises are designed to complement the Maneuvers Manual and the audiovisual presentations. Each exercise is correlated with a specific chapter and section; for example, Exercise 1A applies to Chapter 1, Section A of the Maneuvers Manual.

The workbook contains multiple choice, true/false, matching, and completion exercises. To answer the multiple choice questions, circle the number of the correct choice. Fill in the appropriate blanks to answer the other questions. Further instructions may appear at the beginning of a section or within the body of an individual exercise, when necessary. The answers to all of the exercises are grouped at the back of the manual following the exercises for Chapter 8.

CHAPTER 1 – PRIMARY MANEUVERS

Student Exercise 1A
Straight-And-Level Flight

1. The airplane's altitude and _____ are held constant during straight-and-level flight.

2. Attitude flying is best defined as controlling the airplane's nose and wing positions in reference to the natural _____ .

3. The airplane's pitch attitude can best be controlled by

   1. focusing on a point over the center of the airplane's nose.
   2. concentrating on the altimeter.
   3. selecting a reference point directly in front of the pilot.
   4. selecting a reference point on the ground.

4. A technique used to observe other air traffic and minimize focusing on one reference point is known as _____.

5. Flying is best described as a continuous series of _____ (small, large) corrections.

6. The control surface which controls the pitch attitude or position of the airplane's nose is the _____.

7. When cruise airspeed is set and power is held constant, airspeed will vary only if the _____ _____ changes.

8. Trim tab adjustments should be made to
   1. change the airspeed.
   2. change the pitch attitude.
   3. correct the heading.
   4. remove control wheel pressure.

9. The proper procedure for trimming the airplane is to first set the desired pitch attitude and airspeed, then trim away any _____ _____ necessary to hold that attitude.

10. The turn coordinator which shows coordinated flight is _____.

11. Kinesthetic sense generally is defined as the feel of motion and pressure changes through nerve endings in the organs, muscles, and tendons, and is sometimes described as the "_____-of-the-_____" sensation.

12. A minimum acceptable performance standard for straight-and-level flight includes the requirement to maintain heading, altitude, and airspeed within plus or minus _____ degrees of the assigned heading, _____ feet of the assigned altitude, and _____ knots of the desired airspeed.

Student Exercise 1B
Climbs And Descents

1. Climbs are practiced to develop proficiency in establishing the proper climb _____, applying the appropriate _____ pressures, and _____ the airplane correctly.

2. The proper steps for entering a climb from straight-and-level flight are to

    1. add power, increase back pressure to establish the climb attitude, stabilize desired airspeed.
    2. stabilize desired airspeed, add power, increase back pressure to establish the climb attitude.
    3. increase back pressure to establish the climb attitude, stabilize desired airspeed, and add power.
    4. stabilize desired airspeed, decrease back pressure to establish the climb attitude, and add power.

3. The force which contributes most to the left-turning tendency of an airplane during a climb is

    1. torque.
    2. P-factor.
    3. spiraling slipstream.
    4. positive G loading.

Match the climb speeds listed in questions 4 through 6 with the letter corresponding to the appropriate definition.

4. _____ Cruise climb speed

    a. Results in greatest altitude gain in shortest distance

5. _____ Best rate-of-climb speed

    b. Results in greatest altitude gain per minute

6. _____ Best angle-of-climb speed

    c. Results in best engine cooling and forward visibility

7. The level-off from a 500 f.p.m. rate of climb should begin approximately _____ feet below the desired altitude.

8. Descents are practiced to learn the techniques for losing altitude without gaining excessive _____ , and controlling the rate of descent with power and _____ .

9. Most light training airplanes have power-off glide ratios of approximately 10:1. This means the airplane moves _____ feet forward for every 10 feet of altitude lost.

10. Power additions during a stabilized descent will

    1. increase the rate of descent.
    2. decrease airspeed.
    3. decrease the rate of descent
    4. increase airspeed.

11. _____ (true, false) A maximum range descent is best performed with full flaps.

12. Acceptable performance for climbs and/or descents requires prompt recognition of the correct _____ , and level-offs within _____ feet of the desired altitude.

Student Exercise 1C — Turns

1. In a level turn, the force opposing total lift is a resultant force made up of _____ force and the _____ of the airplane.

2. When initiating a left turn, the control pressures place the left aileron _____ and the right aileron _____.

3. _____ (true, false) The steepness of bank in a turn depends on how long the ailerons are deflected.

4. A coordinated turn requires the simultaneous application of _____ pressure and aileron pressure.

5. _____ (true, false) Adverse yaw is the result of the lift produced by the lowered aileron during a turn.

Complete questions six through eight by matching the turn coordinators with the appropriate descriptions.

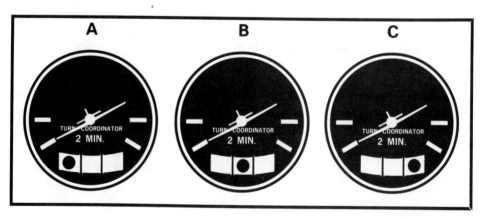

6. _____ Slip

7. _____ Skid

8. _____ Coordinated Turn

9. A _____ - _____ turn produces a turn rate of three degrees per second.

10. _____ (true, false) The angle of bank necessary to produce a standard-rate turn is strictly a function of airspeed; the *lower* the airspeed, the greater the angle of bank required to maintain a standard-rate turn.

11. Performance of a turn is considered acceptable if the selected altitude is maintained within _____ feet and the roll-out is completed within _____ degrees of the preselected heading.

12. A coordination exercise that requires the use of rudder and ailerons in a manner exactly opposite to that used in normal turns is called a _____ _____.

Student Exercise 2A
Preflight Check and
Engine Starting Procedures

1. _____ (true, false) One reason for using a written checklist during preflight is that it makes the transition to a different make or model of airplane easier.

2. The pilot must insure that the airplane performance _____ are displayed or placarded, if no flight manual is provided.

3. An aircraft document or certificate that must be available, but not necessarily onboard the aircraft, is the

    1. airplane radio station license.
    2. aircraft airworthiness certificate.
    3. aircraft registration certificate.
    4. engine logbook.

4. _____ (true, false) The presence of water in a clear container of gasoline can be detected because water is lighter than gasoline and will float on the surface.

5. Propeller nicks of more than approximately _____ - _____ inch in depth should be repaired by a qualified FAA licensed mechanic prior to flight.

6. _____ (true, false) The carburetor heat control is placed in the cold position during start so that air entering the engine is filtered to remove dust and dirt.

7. The primer is used to pump fuel into the engine _____ to aid in starting.

8. _____ (true, false) Prior to starting the engine on a cold day, a thorough look around the propeller eliminates the need for opening a window or door and shouting "clear prop."

9. Excessive friction within the engine after starting can be caused by _____ r.p.m. or _____ oil pressure.

10. If the oil pressure does not register properly within 30 seconds after starting in warm weather, the engine should be _____ _____.

11. After starting an engine in cold weather, the oil pressure should register properly within _____ seconds.

12. _____ (true, false) To avoid damage to the starter motor, it is important to release the starter as soon as the engine starts.

Student Exercise 2B
Taxiing, Engine Shutdown, and Tiedown Procedures

1. Power control is important for correct taxiing. For example, more power is required to _____ (start, keep) the airplane moving than to _____ (start, keep) it moving.

2. Many flight instructors recommend the use of a taxi speed that is equal to a brisk _____.

3. The method used during taxiing to make a smaller radius turn than is possible with nosewheel steering alone is called _____ _____.

4. While taxiing at five knots into a 20-knot headwind, the total wind velocity over the wings is
   1. 10 knots.
   2. 15 knots.
   3. 20 knots.
   4. 25 knots.

5. Most modern light airplanes are steered with the _____ while taxiing.

6. _____ (true, false) Proper control position practice during taxi with a wind is of little or no benefit.

7. _____ (true, false) Although it is good practice to use checklists during preflight and engine starting, there is no need to use a checklist for engine shutdown.

8. _____(true, false) The propeller tip should not be pushed or pulled when moving an airplane.

9. The control surfaces can be damaged during high winds or gusting conditions if the _____ _____ is not used when the aircraft is secured.

Answer questions 10 through 13 by matching the correct control position with the appropriate wind condition encountered during taxi.

10. _____ Slight headwind   a.   Control wheel full left

11. _____ Strong tailwind   b.   Control wheel full forward

12. _____ Right quartering tailwind   c.   Control wheel neutral

13. _____ Left quartering headwind   d.   Control wheel full left and forward

Student Exercise 2C
Traffic Patterns

1. The direction of turn in a non-standard traffic pattern is to the _____.

Complete the exercise below by placing the correct letter identifying the traffic pattern segments next to the identifying names.

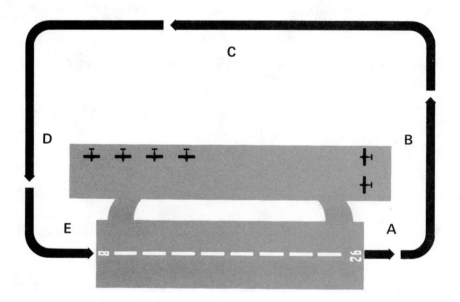

2. _____ Takeoff (upwind) leg

3. _____ Base leg

4. _____ Downwind leg

5. _____ Final approach leg

6. _____ Crosswind leg

7. _____ (true, false) The normal procedure is to enter the traffic pattern at a 45° angle to the downwind leg, abeam the midpoint of the runway.

8. Traffic patterns at uncontrolled airports normally are entered on the

    1. downwind leg.
    2. crosswind leg.
    3. base leg.
    4. upwind or takeoff leg.

9. To make an aircraft more clearly visible during periods of reduced visibility or bright sunlight the _____ - _____ and _____ lights should be turned on.

10. _____ (true, false) The scan for other aircraft should be accomplished by sectors, rather than permitting the eyes to sweep across the sky.

11. _____ (true, false) The pilot is relieved of the responsibility of seeing and avoiding other traffic while operating under radar control within a terminal control area.

12. The traffic pattern altitude at most airports is _____ feet above the airport elevation.

Student Exercise 3A
Tracking a Straight Line and Constant Radius Turns

Match the lettered terms with the related statements one through three.

1. _____ Path of an airplane over the ground while flying
   a straight line

   a. Heading

2. _____ Wind correction angle used to correct for drift

   b. Track

3. _____ Airplane's magnetic direction

   c. Crab

4. While tracking a straight line, the magnitude of the crab angle depends on the wind _____ and _____ .

5. For ground reference maneuvers, the wind correction angle is determined by a

   1. flight computer.
   2. trial-and-error method.
   3. wind sock.
   4. coordinated drift method.

6. To keep the radius of turn constant in a wind, it is necessary to vary the

   1. angle of bank.
   2. groundspeed.
   3. airspeed.
   4. crab angle.

7. _____ (true, false) A turn performed at a constant angle of bank in a headwind will inscribe a circular track over the ground and be completed at the point where it began.

8. The steepest angle of bank in a constant radius turn will occur at the point of greatest _____ (groundspeed, airspeed).

9. If the pilot looks out the side window on the downwind side in a constant radius turn, the center of the circle appears _____ (ahead, behind) the lateral axis.

Complete the exercise below by placing the correct letter next to the appropriate description.

10. _____ crab toward reference point

11. _____ crab away from reference point

12. _____ steepest angle of bank

13. _____ shallowest angle of bank

14. _____ fastest groundspeed

15. _____ slowest groundspeed

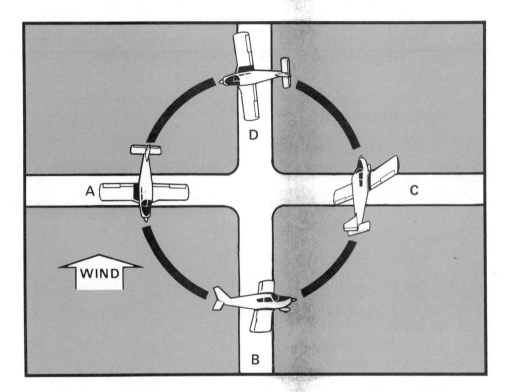

Student Exercise 3B
Rectangular Courses And Elementary Eights

1. Rectangular courses provide practice in tracking and evaluating _____ angle.

2. The determining factor in selecting the distance from the field boundary when performing rectangular courses should be the normal distance from the runway of the _____ leg of a typical airport traffic pattern.

3. _____ (true, false) Wind blowing diagonally across a rectangular course requires a crab angle on all four legs.

4. Elementary eights consist of "eights _____ a road," "eights _____ a road," and eights _____ pylons."

5. The ground track for elementary eights should be in the form of a _____ _____ .

6. _____ (true, false) In performing eights across a road, the airplane should cross the point which forms the center of the "8" in straight-and-level flight.

7. _____ (true, false) The steepest bank when performing eights across a road occurs when the airspeed is highest.

8. In eights around pylons, the angle of bank should not exceed
    1. 20°.
    2. 30°.
    3. 45°.
    4. 60°.

9. The turning portion of eights around pylons closely resembles the maneuver called
    1. "S" turns.
    2. turns about a point.
    3. eights along a road.
    4. steep power turns.

10. _____ (true, false) For acceptable performance of elementary eights, deviation from the selected altitude should not exceed 200 feet.

Student Exercise 3C
S-Turns Across A Road
And Turns About A Point

1. One objective when flying S-turns across a road is to complete two perfect half _____ of equal size on _____ sides of the road.

Complete questions two through seven by placing the correct letter or letters next to the identifying description.

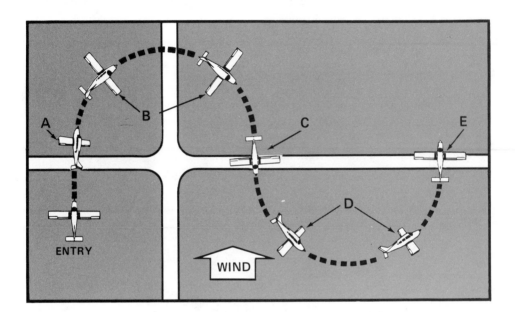

2. _____ Fastest groundspeed

3. _____ Slowest groundspeed

4. _____ Bank gradually steepened

5. _____ Bank gradually reduced

6. _____ Aircraft level

7. _____ Steepest bank angle

8. _____ (true, false) Turns about a point require constant radius turns be flown while maintaining a constant altitude.

9. _____ (true, false) A telephone pole or tree provides a better reference point for turns about a point than a road intersection.

10. _____ (true, false) Flight below the minimum safe altitude prescribed by regulations, or excessively steep banks during turns about a point, are disqualifying on a flight test.

Student Exercise 4A — Slips

1. The flight attitude used to increase the angle of descent without causing an increase in airspeed is a _____ .

2. _____ (true, false) Flaps serve the same purpose as a slip during a landing.

3. To initiate a forward slip, one wing is lowered using aileron control, and opposite rudder is applied simultaneously to keep the airplane from turning in the direction of the _____ wing.

4. To prevent the airspeed from increasing when executing a slip, the nose is positioned slightly _____ the normal gliding position.

5. _____ (true, false) The engine should be at cruise power during a forward slip to prevent a stall.

6. The _____ slip normally is used to compensate for drift during crosswind landings.

7. _____ (true, false) The nose of the airplane, during a side slip in a no-wind condition, remains on the same heading throughout the maneuver.

8. _____ (true, false) The airplane's ground track during a side slip in a no-wind condition is a straight line parallel to the longitudinal axis of the airplane.

Student Exercise 4B
Normal And Crosswind Takeoffs

1. _____ (true, false) It is not necessary to perform the pretakeoff check if you are in a hurry since the engine has had ample time to warm up during taxi.

2. When carburetor heat is applied during the pretakeoff check, the engine r.p.m. will _____ , indicating that carburetor heat is working.

3. The appropriate procedure for checking the traffic pattern at an uncontrolled field is to
   1. call the tower for traffic and winds.
   2. call UNICOM for traffic and winds.
   3. receive clearance from ground control before taking the runway.
   4. make a 360° taxi turn in the direction of the traffic pattern to observe the entire area for traffic.

4. Directional control during the takeoff roll is maintained with

    1. differential braking.
    2. power.
    3. rudder.
    4. aileron.

5. The wind that acts at right angles to the airplane's path on takeoff or landing is called the _____ _____ .

Using the maximum safe crosswind chart, answer questions six through nine by stating whether the wind conditions are safe or unsafe for takeoff.

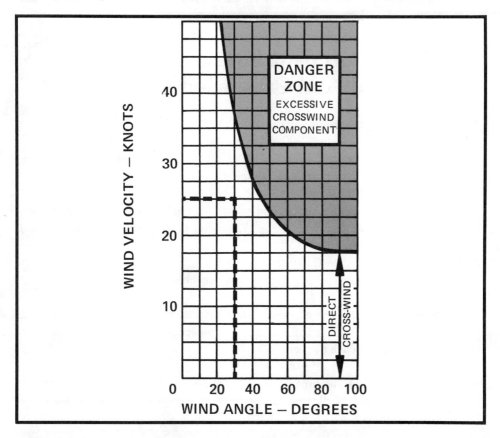

Question	Wind Velocity	Wind Correction Angle	Safe or Unsafe
6.	30 kts.	20°	
7.	20 kts.	70°	
8.	18 kts.	90°	
9.	15 kts.	40°	

10. _____ (true, false) It is common to initially use full aileron deflection on a crosswind takeoff roll due to the ineffectiveness of the flight controls at slow airspeeds.

11. The correct flight control positions during takeoff with a right crosswind are

    1. control wheel left and rudder right.
    2. control wheel left and rudder left.
    3. control wheel right and rudder right.
    4. control wheel right and rudder left.

12. A straight-ahead landing is the only choice if power is lost just after takeoff and the plane is below _____ feet AGL.

Student Exerise 4C
Normal And Crosswind Landings

1. Planning for a landing begins on the _____ leg of the traffic pattern.

2. During an approach to landing, _____ controls the rate of descent, while _____ controls the airspeed.

3. The airplane's track over the ground should be approximately one-half mile and parallel to the runway on the _____ leg of the traffic pattern.

4. At the 180° point in the traffic pattern, the _____ is reduced and the airspeed is allowed to _____ to approach speed.

5. An assessment of altitude, airspeed, distance from the runway, and wind is made at the _____ _____ to determine whether corrections must be made in the approach pattern.

6. _____ (true, false) The turn to final should be made at approximately 400 feet AGL, and it should be planned so the airplane rolls out on an extension of the runway centerline.

7. _____ (true, false) It is important to remember that an airplane turning from the base leg to final has the right of way over any aircraft on final.

8. _____ (true, false) The runway will appear to shorten and become wider during a steep approach.

9. _____ (true, false) The apparent shape of the runway remains fixed if a constant approach angle is maintained.

10. _____ (true, false) The approach speed is frequently near the best angle-of-glide speed. This means any other airspeed will result in a higher rate of descent.

11. Changing the attitude of the airplane from a glide or descent attitude to a landing attitude is called the _____ .

12. The flareout for most training airplanes begins at approximately
    1.   5 feet AGL.
    2.   15 feet AGL.
    3.   40 feet AGL.
    4.   50 feet AGL.

13. Sighting over the center of the nose during landing tends to cause the airplane to land in a _____ , which places heavy _____ loads on the landing gear.

14. _____ (true, false) The extension of wing flaps increases both lift and drag, and provides a slower approach airspeed than without flaps.

15. _____ (true, false) A go-around is executed by adding full throttle, accelerating to best rate-of-climb speed, and slowly raising the flaps.

16. The rate of descent on a no-flap landing normally is _____ (greater, less) than when partial flaps are used, and the approach tends to be _____ (steeper, shallower).

17. Use of full flaps produces a _____ rate of descent, _____ touchdown speed, and a _____ ground roll.

18. On final, during a crosswind landing, the _____ is lowered into the wind and opposite _____ pressure is used to keep the nose pointed straight down the runway.

19. _____ (true, false) It is normal for the airplane to touch down on one wheel during a crosswind landing to prevent it from drifting to either side.

Student Exercise 5A
Minimum Controllable Airspeed

1. _____ (true, false) An objective of flight at minimum controllable airspeed is to learn the relationship of power to altitude and attitude to airspeed.

2. Minimum controllable airspeed must be sufficiently slow so that any _____ (increase, decrease) in speed or _____ (increase, decrease) in load factor will result in the immediate indications of a stall.

3. The proper technique for reducing airspeed for flight at minimum controllable airspeed is to

    1. begin a climb to allow airspeed to decay slowly.
    2. reduce power and begin a climb.
    3. reduce power then apply back pressure to maintain altitude.
    4. lower flaps while reducing power.

4. When an airplane is slowed and power is applied, the resulting left-turning tendency is caused by

    1. low angle of attack.
    2. P-factor.
    3. decreased airspeed.
    4. the decrease in spiral slipstream.

5. _____ (true, false) Control effectiveness is decreased during flight at minimum controllable airspeed due to reduced relative wind velocity.

6. _____ (true, false) The correct procedure for gaining altitude while flying at minimum controllable airspeed is to apply power.

7. _____ (true, false) Sudden retraction of the flaps during flight at minimum controllable airspeed may place the airplane near or below the stall speed.

8. Acceptable performance during straight-and-level flight at minimum controllable airspeed, requires that altitude be maintained within _____ feet and heading within _____ degrees of that assigned.

Student Exercise 5B
Power-Off Stalls

1. _____ (true, false) One objective for practicing stalls is to acquaint the pilot with the stall warning and handling characteristics as the airplane approaches a stall.

2. According to FAR Part 23, a pilot must be able to prevent more than _____° of roll or _____° of yaw through normal use of controls during the recovery from a stall.

3. A stall is caused by an excessive angle of attack which causes the smooth airflow over the upper wing surface to break away, resulting in a loss of _____.

4. The angle of attack is the angle between the wing _____ line and the _____ wind.

5. _____ (true, false) An airplane can stall only at its published stall speed while at the critical angle of attack.

6. The marking on the airspeed indicator that shows the power-off stall speed with the landing gear down and flaps fully extended is the low speed end of the _____ arc.

7. The marking on the airspeed indicator that shows the power-off stall speed with the landing gear up and flaps retracted is the low speed end of the _____ arc.

8. An increase in the angle of bank will _____ (increase, decrease) the stall speed, while extension of flaps will _____ (increase, decrease) the stall speed.

9. Stall warnings begin 5 to 10 knots before the stall speed and are indicated by
   1. loud and intense slipstream noises.
   2. lighter control pressures.
   3. buffeting of the controls.
   4. fluctuating airspeed indications.

10. _____ (true, false) The recovery from a full stall begins after the nose pitches down; whereas recovery from an imminent stall is initiated at the first indication of a stall.

11. The first action in a stall recovery is to _____ the angle of attack by releasing back pressure, while simultaneously applying full _____.

Student Exercise 5C — Steep Turns

1. _____ (true, false) The increase in angle of bank during steep turns causes the stall speed to decrease as altitude is maintained.

2. If a steep turn is entered too rapidly, the pilot probably will experience difficulty controlling _____ (angle-of-bank, altitude).

3. _____ (true, false) Elevator control pressure can be relieved during steep turns by using trim.

4. _____ (true, false) When seated in the left seat, the nose of the airplane seems to be considerably lower in a steep turn to the right than in a left turn.

5. To correct for a loss of altitude during a steep turn, _____ the angle of bank temporarily and simultaneously _____ the pitch attitude.

6. How many degrees before reaching the desired heading should the rollout begin during steep turns?

   1. 10°
   2. 20°
   3. 30°
   4. 40°

7. _____ (true, false) The overbanking tendency during steep turns is more evident in a right turn than in a left turn.

Student Exercise 6A
Power-On and Accelerated
Maneuver Stalls

1. _____ (true, false) One of the primary goals when practicing stalls is learning to recognize the changing control responses as an airplane approaches a stall.

2. _____ (true, false) Since climb power is used during practice of the takeoff stalls, they should be entered from a high airspeed.

3. _____ (true, false) Left rudder pressure is required as the power and pitch attitude are increased during the power-on stall.

4. To recover from a power-on stall, the pilot should apply full power and simultaneously _____ the angle of attack.

5. The recommended bank angles for practicing power-on turning stalls are from _____° to _____°.

6. _____ (true, false) Flaps are normally extended during the demonstration of accelerated maneuver stalls .

7. _____ (true, false) The rapid retraction of flaps during stall recoveries can induce a secondary stall or a high rate of descent.

8. _____ (true, false) The term "accelerated" describes the rapidity with which the stall is induced.

9. The most likely type of spin that pilots will encounter in training airplanes is called a _____ - _____ spin.

10. The three possible pitch attitudes the airplane can assume during the spin rotation are _____ , _____ , and _____ .

11. _____ (true, false) No matter what the make or model of airplane, the spin recovery technique always remains the same.

Student Exercise 6B
Maximum Performance Takeoffs
And Landings

1. The best _____ -of-climb airspeed provides the greatest altitude gain in the shortest distance traveled.

2. The best _____ -of-climb airspeed provides the greatest altitude gain in the shortest time.

3. _____ (true, false) The obstructions on each end of the runway that must be cleared during short-field practice sessions normally are assumed to be 50 feet in height.

4. Back pressure is applied for liftoff on a short-field takeoff, immediately prior to reaching the best

    1. rate-of-climb airspeed.
    2. cruise-climb airspeed.
    3. angle-of-climb airspeed.
    4. takeoff speed.

5. Short-field landings normally are executed with flaps in the _____ _____ position.

6. _____ (true, false) The final approach for a short-field landing should be at a constant glide angle.

7. _____ (true, false) Flaps should be left down after touchdown to increase drag and braking action.

8. One objective of the soft-field takeoff is to transfer the weight of the airplane from the main landing gear to the _____ as quickly and smoothly as possible.

9. _____ (true, false) The soft-field takeoff procedure requires accelerating the airplane in a nose-high attitude with the nosewheel clear of the surface during most of the takeoff ground run.

10. After liftoff from a soft-field, the pitch altitude is reduced gradually to allow the airplane to accelerate in _____ _____ to the normal climb airspeed.

11. The soft-field takeoff procedure actually begins during the _____ (runup, taxi) phase.

12. When close to the runway during landing, an airplane may temporarily gain lift from a phenomenon known as _____ _____ .

13. _____ (true, false) The nosewheel should be held clear of the soft runway surface during touchdown and roll-out to reduce the possibility of an abrupt stop.

Student Exercise 6C
Emergency Landing Procedures

1. Number the following steps in the proper sequence for the execution of an emergency landing.

   _____ Attempt to determine the cause of the power failure and restart the engine, if possible.

   _____ Establish the best glide speed.

   _____ Establish a landing approach to the selected field.

   _____ Turn to a heading that will take the airplane to the selected field.

   _____ Scan the immediate area for a suitable field.

2. _____ (true, false) Flaps should be used to maintain the best power-off glide speed.

3. _____ (true, false) During an emergency landing, it is advisable to circle away from the field rather then try to make a long, straight-in glide.

4. Sudden engine power loss normally is caused by _____ (oil, fuel) problems.

5. Ideally, during an emergency landing the airplane should be at the _____° point (above the intended point of touchdown) when normal traffic pattern altitude is reached.

6. _____ (true, false) Flaps should be used as required during the emergency landing approach.

7. When the emergency landing approach is executed properly, it will appear that the airplane will touch down _____ of the intended point of landing.

CHAPTER 7 — ATTITUDE INSTRUMENT FLYING

1. Three fundamental skills used in all instrument flight maneuvers are instrument cross check, instrument _____ , and airplane _____ .

2. The instrument which replaces the natural horizon during instrument flight is the _____ indicator.

3. _____ (true, false) The attitude indicator provides the information necessary for flight during instrument conditions.

4. The continuous systematic observation of the flight instruments during instrument flight is known as _____ _____ , or _____ .

5. The natural human inclination to observe a specific instrument accurately results in _____ .

6. _____ (true, false) Because of conflicting sensations from the inner ear and postural sense, the pilot must learn to trust the flight instruments.

7. Which primary flight instrument is used for bank control?
    1. Turn coordinator
    2. Heading indicator
    3. Attitude indicator
    4. Magnetic compass

8. The flight instrument that provides a pictorial display of the airplane's overall attitude is the
    1. altimeter.
    2. vertical velocity indicator.
    3. attitude indicator.
    4. heading indicator.

9. _____ (true, false) A good tight grip on the control wheel insures smooth and precise attitude control.

10. _____ (true, false) A full bar width adjustment on the attitude indicator should be made for a 500-foot altitude correction.

11. _____ (true, false) The vertical velocity indicator is a good trend instrument because it indicates the direction of pitch change almost instantaneously.

12. The attitude indicator is the primary bank control instrument during a turn, while the _____ (heading, airspeed) indicator and turn _____ are supporting instruments.

13. _____ (true, false) A 360° standard-rate turn to the left will take two minutes to complete.

14. _____(true, false) For a constant-rate descent at a specified airspeed, the vertical velocity indicator becomes the principal quality instrument for pitch.

15. _____ (true, false) The normal lead for a leveloff from a climb or descent is 20 percent of the vertical velocity indication.

16. To determine the amount of lead required to roll-out from a turn, use approximately _____ - _____ the angle of bank.

17. To recover from a nose-high critical attitude, a pilot should simultaneously decrease _____ to reduce angle of attack, _____ power, and roll the wings _____ . (See accompanying illustration.)

18. The immediate concern during the recovery from a nose-low critical attitude is

    1. exceeding the limit load factor.
    2. leveling the wings.
    3. excessive airspeed.
    4. retracting the flaps.

CHAPTER 8 — NIGHT FLYING

1. _____ (true, false) A night preflight inspection should be much more stringent than a day preflight.

2. A red position light is located on the _____ wing, a _____ position light on the tail, and a green position light on the _____ wing.

3. _____ (true, false) Taxi and landing lights should not be checked during preflight because of the high energy drain on the battery.

4. _____ (true, false) A white strobe light may be used as an anti-collision light in place of a red rotating beacon.

5. To provide an alternate source of light if the interior lights malfunction a _____ should be carried during night flights.

6. Military airports can be distinguished from civil airports because their beacons emit two _____ flashes alternating with a single _____ flash.

For questions 7 through 10, list the color of lights associated with each airport part.

7. _____ Runway   9. _____ Threshold

8. _____ Taxiway   10. _____ Obstructions or unusable areas

11. _____ (true, false) In addition to calling "clear prop," the landing light or position lights can be momentarily turned on to warn others the propeller is about to rotate.

12. If the intensity of lighting equipment drops when engine r.p.m. is reduced, a weak _____ may be indicated.

13. A night takeoff may require the use of instruments as the normal ground _____ disappear.

14. _____ (true, false) Except in an emergency, a night landing should never be attempted without the landing light illuminated.

Using the VASI indicators below, answer questions 15 through 17.

LIGHT BARS ALL WHITE	LIGHT BARS RED OVER WHITE	LIGHT BARS ALL RED
A	B	C

15. ___ Below glide path   16. ___ On proper glide path   17. ___ Above glide path

WORKBOOK ANSWER SECTION

━━━━ CHAPTER 1 — ANSWERS PRIMARY MANEUVERS ━━━━

STUDENT EXERCISE 1A ANSWERS

1. heading
2. horizon
3. 3
4. scanning
5. small
6. elevator
7. pitch attitude or nose position
8. 4
9. control pressure
10. C
11. seat, pants
12. 10, 100, 5

STUDENT EXERCISE 1B ANSWERS

1. attitude, control, trimming
2. 3
3. 2
4. C
5. B

6. A
7. 50
8. airspeed, attitude
9. 100
10. 3
11. false
12. attitude, 100

STUDENT EXERCISE 1C ANSWERS

1. centrifugal, weight
2. up, down
3. true
4. rudder
5. true
6. A
7. C
8. B
9. standard-rate
10. false
11. 100, 20
12. Dutch roll

━━━ CHAPTER 2 — ANSWERS AIRPLANE GROUND OPERATIONS ━━━
AND TRAFFIC PATTERNS

STUDENT EXERCISE 2A ANSWERS

1. true
2. limitations
3. 4
4. false
5. one-eighth
6. true
7. cylinders
8. false
9. high, low
10. shut down
11. 60
12. true

STUDENT EXERCISE 2B ANSWERS

1. start, keep
2. walk
3. differential braking
4. 4
5. nosewheel
6. false

7. false
8. true
9. control lock
10. C
11. B
12. D
13. A

STUDENT EXERCISE 2C ANSWERS

1. right
2. A
3. D
4. C
5. E
6. B
7. true
8. 1
9. anti-collision, landing
10. true
11. false
12. 1,000

CHAPTER 3 — ANSWERS GROUND REFERENCE MANEUVERS

STUDENT EXERCISE 3A ANSWERS
1. B
2. C
3. A
4. speed, direction
5. 2
6. 1
7. false
8. groundspeed
9. ahead
10. D
11. B
12. C
13. A
14. C
15. A

STUDENT EXERCISE 3B ANSWERS
1. crab
2. downwind

3. true
4. along, across, around
5. figure eight
6. true
7. false
8. 3
9. 2
10. false

STUDENT EXERCISE 3C ANSWERS
1. circles, opposite
2. A, E
3. C
4. D
5. B
6. C, E
7. A
8. true
9. false
10. true

CHAPTER 4 — ANSWERS SLIPS, TAKEOFFS, AND LANDINGS

STUDENT EXERCISE 4A ANSWERS
1. slip
2. true
3. lowered
4. above
5. false
6. side
7. true
8. false

STUDENT EXERCISE 4B ANSWERS
1. false
2. drop
3. 4
4. 3
5. crosswind component
6. safe
7. unsafe
8. unsafe
9. safe
10. true

11. 4
12. 400

STUDENT EXERCISE 4C ANSWERS
1. downwind
2. power, attitude
3. downwind
4. power, slow
5. key position
6. true
7. false
8. false
9. true
10. true
11. flareout
12. 2
13. crab, side
14. true
15. false
16. less, shallower
17. higher, slower, shorter
18. wing, rudder
19. true

CHAPTER 5 — ANSWERS ADVANCED MANEUVERS

STUDENT EXERCISE 5A ANSWERS

1. true
2. decrease, increase
3. 3
4. 2
5. true
6. true
7. true
8. 100, 10

STUDENT EXERCISE 5B ANSWERS

1. true
2. 15°, 15°
3. lift
4. chord, relative

5. false
6. white
7. green
8. increase, decrease
9. 3
10. true
11. reduce, power (throttle)

STUDENT EXERCISE 5C ANSWERS

1. false
2. altitude
3. true
4. true
5. reduce, increase
6. 2
7. false

CHAPTER 6 — ANSWERS ADVANCED FLIGHT OPERATIONS

STUDENT EXERCISE 6A ANSWERS

1. true
2. false
3. false
4. decrease
5. 15, 20
6. false
7. true
8. false
9. nose-low
10. inverted, flat, nose-low
11. false

STUDENT EXERCISE 6B ANSWERS

1. angle
2. rate
3. true
4. 3
5. fully extended
6. true

7. false
8. wings
9. true
10. ground effect
11. taxi
12. ground effect
13. true

STUDENT EXERCISE 6C ANSWERS

1. D
   A
   E
   C
   B
2. false
3. false
4. fuel
5. 180
6. true
7. short

——— CHAPTER 7 — ANSWERS ATTITUDE INSTRUMENT FLYING ———

STUDENT EXERCISE 7 ANSWERS

1. interpretation, control
2. attitude
3. false
4. cross checking or scanning
5. fixation
6. true
7. 3
8. 3
9. false
10. true
11. true
12. heading, coordinator
13. true
14. true
15. false
16. one-half
17. pitch, increase, level
18. 3

——— CHAPTER 8 — ANSWERS NIGHT FLYING ———

STUDENT EXERCISE 8 ANSWERS

1. false
2. left, white, right
3. false
4. true
5. flashlight
6. white, green
7. white
8. blue
9. green
10. red
11. true
12. battery
13. references
14. false
15. C
16. B
17. A

ALPHABETICAL INDEX

D

E

F

G

H

I